LIFE, DEATH & BEYOND

LIFE, DEATH & BEYOND

J. Kerby Anderson

ZONDERVAN
PUBLISHING HOUSE OF THE ZONDERVAN CORPORATION
GRAND RAPIDS, MICHIGAN 49506

Lᴉꜰᴇ, Dᴇᴀᴛʜ ᴀɴᴅ Bᴇʏᴏɴᴅ
Copyright © 1980 by The Zondervan Corporation

Library of Congress Cataloging in Publication Data

Anderson, John Kerby, 1951-
  Life, death and beyond.

  Bibliography: p.
  Includes index.
   1. Death.   2. Death—Biblical teaching.
  3. Future life.   4. Future life—Biblical teaching.
  I. Title.
  BT825.A48   248.8'6   79-28128
  ISBN 0-310-41571-3

Printed in the United States of America

Material from *Beyond Death's Door*, © 1978, reprinted by permission of Thomas Nelson, Inc., Nashville, Tennessee.
Material from *Oregon's Amazing Miracle*, © 1976, reprinted by permission of Christ for the Nations, Dallas, Texas.

Scripture quotations are from the Holy Bible, New International Version, copyright © 1978 by New York International Bible Society.

*To my wife, Susanne, for her patience and
encouragement in a film and writing project
that has lasted for more than a year
and
to my daughter, Amy, who waited to be born
until the day after I sent the completed
manuscript to the publisher.*

CONTENTS

ONE

DEATH
IN OUR
DAY

The hospital doors burst open, and in rushed a doctor followed by a team of nurses and equipment. They joined an already-busy group of nurses and aides attempting to revive a patient. The doctor ordered an injection. There was no effect. He grabbed the shock machine and placed the plates on the patient. The patient jumped from the shock, but there was no response on the electrocardiogram. There was no hope. They had fought another battle with death and lost.

Such a scene is not uncommon in modern hospitals. The battle with death is a daily occurrence. Some may not die in the midst of such sophisticated technology, but all of us die. Death is the most universal and most democratic of all human functions. It strikes people at any time with little respect for age, class, creed, or color.

Unlike most of the major transitions of our lives, death is a uniquely individual event. Each society has certain institutionalized ceremonies, known as *rites de passage*, to mark a change in status or a moment of transition. The change might be biological, at one's birth or the longer passage into adulthood. It might also be social, as in marriage or inheritance.

But in every case, except death, the individual enters this new status with others. Death is a solitary passage in time.

Not only is death universal and solitary, but it is compulsory. Except in the case of suicide, no one can control when he will die. When death comes, we must submit. In his book, *Death of Man*, Edwin Shneidman observes,

> We must face the fact that death is the one act in which man is forced to engage. The word "forced" has a special meaning here. It implies that death, like torture, rape, capital punishment, kidnap, lobotomy, and other degradation ceremonies is a form of coercion and impressment. The threat of being erased, of being reduced to nothingness can be viewed reasonably only as the most perfidious of forced punishment.[1]

The Ultimate Question

Man's ultimate destiny is to die. But it has always been hard for him to accept this ultimate fate. Historically, man has been defined as a death-denying creature. But this is difficult to understand. For if he knows he is going to die someday, he should be able to accept it and resolve the tensions surrounding death. As Arnold Toynbee, the philosopher and historian, has put it:

> Man alone . . . has foreknowledge of his coming death . . . and, possessing this foreknowledge, has a chance, if he chooses to take it, of pondering over the strangeness of his destiny. . . . [He] has at least a possibility of coping with it, since he is endowed with the capacity to think about it in advance and . . . to face it and to deal with it in some way that is worthy of human dignity.[2]

Though man should face the prospect of his own mortality, he rarely does. Every day we receive fresh reminders about death. In the newspapers we read of tragedies involving loss of life. On television we see acts or the results of acts of war and terrorism. Even on the stage and screen we watch scenes involving forms of violence. But rarely do we connect the violence we see with our own personal situation.

Death is something that seems to happen only to someone else. When death strikes someone close to us, there seems to be a mechanism that prevents us from seeing its future consequences for us. Highway death tolls never seem to strike us as personal threats. We avoid the personal significance of death as we hold to a naive form of personal immortality.

Not only is such a view unrealistic, it is also potentially harmful to us psychologically. Much of the psychic distress of modern man has been attributed to his fear of death. In his book *The Denial of Death* the late Ernest Becker leaves little doubt that it is not unresolved sexuality that is the psychological problem of man. Instead it is the *repression* of the knowledge of death that is the source of most human anxiety.[3]

Dr. Rollo May, a psychoanalyst in New York, has come to a similar conclusion. He has had to revise his previous thinking in the light of his findings in psychoanalysis. He believes that it is death and not sex that is the basic cause of man's psychic disorders.[4] In fact one psychoanalyst has even gone so far to say that every fear is ultimately a fear of death.[5] While this view may seem too extreme, it does point out the growing evidence that a proper view of death is one of the greatest needs of man in the twentieth century.

In recent years, there has been an increased interest in the topic of death. It was one of the topics that used to be avoided at cocktail parties and other social occasions, but it is now a topic that is in vogue in our society. The subject of life and death is one of the most popular subjects of discussion.

Breaking Down the Death Barrier

The shift from the denial of death to the discussion of death has been a relatively rapid one. For example, in the April 1970 article on death in America in *Newsweek* magazine, the writer was lamenting the fact that America was a death-denying culture. Eight years later, the May 1978 cover of *Newsweek*, titled "Living With Dying," heralded the new-found interest in the subject of thanatology.*

There are four major reasons for this increased interest in the subject of death. First, the death barrier was broken by the medical profession. Books like *On Death and Dying* and *Questions and Answers on Death and Dying* by Elisabeth Kubler-Ross focused the attention of the medical world on the problems of dying patients. Her work in the mid-sixties began with her desire to interview dying patients for a class she was teaching. After searching the school's six-hundred bed hospital, she found that none of the staff would admit they had a terminally ill patient.

Medical schools used to avoid the topic of death. The staff might treat the dying patient but would ignore the fact of approaching death. Kubler-Ross's books, medical seminars, and public talks did a great deal to break down the death barrier constructed by the medical community. There is, however, further work to be done. A recent survey of 107 medical schools prepared by the Foundation of Thanatology at Columbia Presbyterian Medical Center in New York has shown that only seven schools had a full-term course on death.[6]

Education was the second major force to dismantle the death barrier. In the past few years there has been a very rapid growth in the number of death-education courses in high schools and colleges. In high school it is usually introduced as part of a program in the social studies. In others, like Elk Grove High School in Illinois, the topic of death is addressed in an introductory psychology class. At Miami Beach Senior High School it is part of the English department's cur-

---

*Thanatology is the study of death. The word is based on the Greek word *thanatos*, "death."

riculum. The students read the works of great authors on death, write papers, give oral reports, and even go on field trips to mortuaries.[7]

In college the interest in death is also very high. The interest in the subject of death caught many by surprise. Thanatologist Edwin Shneidman found that the first time he taught a course on death at Harvard, two hundred undergraduates from Radcliffe and Harvard showed up in a classroom that could seat only twenty.[8] Since then, colleges everywhere have been setting up courses, seminars, and colloquia dealing with topics like death, dying, grief, immortality, suicide, and euthanasia. At one university at which I have spoken, the course on death is so popular that there is a waiting list. Students are signing up in order to try to register for the course later in the year.

A third reason for the breakdown of the death barrier was the media. People in the arts have always seen the subject of death as fertile ground for movies and plays. Woody Allen probed its meaning in *Love and Death,* while Ingmar Bergman underscored its horror in *The Seventh Seal,* and Sydney Pollack offered it as the only reasonable alternative to modern despair in his movie *They Shoot Horses, Don't They?*

But now books, newsmagazines, and television are talking about death. Where once death was a subject considered taboo, it is now a hot selling item. Books, magazines, and programs on death are everywhere. Cover stories on death have appeared in *Time, Newsweek, Psychology Today, McCall's, National Observer,* and *Harper's Weekly.*[9]

Before its demise, the *Chicago Daily News* began running a twice-a-month column by Jory Graham on the subject of death. The column, entitled "A Time to Live," was written for those faced with death as well as for members of the dying patient's family. It was so successful that it was picked up for syndication by many newspapers.

A fourth and final reason was public interest. Although the medical profession, education, and the media cleared the path for discussion, it already found an interested public. In his book *New Meanings of Death*—an update of his book *The Meaning of Death*, published eighteen years earlier—Herman Feifel discusses some of the reasons why our society has become so interested in death since the publication of his first book. Though he notes it is still difficult for our society to cope with death, he sees three reasons for the increased interest in the subject of death.

First, the recent advances in innovative medical technology are changing the nature of dying. Patients are being kept "alive" by the use of respirators, intravenous fluids, and repeated cardiac defibrillation or massage. This has focused our attention on death and its definition.

Second, our impersonal technology is alienating us from traditional moorings and is weakening institutional and community supports. This has led to increased loneliness, anxiety, and self-probing.

Third, there has been a growing pessimism concerning the future of humanity. The concern that people may unwittingly or intentionally destroy the balance of nature or bring total global annihilation through nuclear devices is always present. No longer is it possible for human beings to guarantee themselves a sense of immortality through their contribution to society, since it is possible that history may die just as they do.

Never has there been a time in the twentieth century when people are more ready to investigate the subject of death. Not only is there an intense interest in death, but there are many new things to be learned. Psychological and medical advances have helped us learn a great deal about death and the world beyond.

In this book we will be looking at some of these interesting topics. First, we will look at dying in an effort to understand what it is like psychologically for a patient to die. Second, we will look at death and the grieving process in order to investigate man's responses to death, analyze some of the stages of grief, and learn how to comfort the bereaved. Third, we will look at the claims of life after death that have been made by people on their deathbeds and by patients who have "died" and been resuscitated. We will look at these claims and analyze them in light of our knowledge of physiology, pharmacology, and psychology. Finally, we will look at a spiritual analysis of this material in an effort to develop a comprehensive view of life, death, and the world beyond.

TWO

DEALING
WITH
DYING

In the third voyage of *Gulliver's Travels*, Gulliver came upon people who were fated not to die. While we might suppose they would have been happy people, they were not. In fact, the happy people he found were those who knew they were going to die.

Although the thought of living forever may not be too appealing to us, neither is the thought of dying. We may look forward to another life, but we do not look forward to dying. It has been found that most people fear the process of dying much more than they fear death itself.[1] In spite of all our advances in medical technology, we have not been able to lessen man's fear of dying. What we need are people who can tell us reliably about dying, people who can lead us unafraid to our graves.

Research Into Dying

As has already been noted, the death barrier was broken in the late sixties and early seventies. In England, one of the more important books to make the breakthrough was *Dying* by

John Hinton. His practical experience and thorough research into the topics of death, dying, and mourning made it a significant contribution to the field of thanatology.

In the United States, the most significant personality is Elisabeth Kubler-Ross. Any work in the field would be shallow if it did not mention her name. She is not only a pioneer in the field of thanatology but is a distinguished spokeswoman for the medical profession. Her influence is so profound that most books on dying are usually classified as pre-1969 or post-1969 (the date of the publication of her book *On Death and Dying*). The compassion and openness in her first book, as well as her clinical description of the stages of dying, won her wide acclaim from her colleagues.

Her openness toward the dying reflects her experiences as a child in rural Switzerland. In those communities, death was confronted with honesty and dignity. Such experiences gave her great compassion for the dying.

But compassion has always been a hallmark of her life. Even before she entered medical school in Switzerland, she worked with survivors of World War II in eastern Europe. After she became a psychiatrist, she worked first with schizophrenics and then with retarded children who were deaf, dumb, or blind. In the last decade, she has been working with dying patients and their families.

Because of her work with so many dying patients, she gained a valuable perspective on the experience of dying and grief. Although she was not the first to describe the stages of dying, she certainly was the first to publicize them extensively to the medical world and the general public. Her first book, *On Death and Dying*, is filled not only with much important clinical information, but also with sensitivity, compassion, and candor. One cannot read the book and not be struck by the harmonious blend of intellect and emotion, of medicine and mercy.

Stages of Dying

Most books and articles on dying describe many of the stages or phases of dying. In her book, Kubler-Ross describes five psychological stages of dying, and since these are most familiar, we will look at them in detail. Her deliniation of the stages of dying is not endorsed by all researchers but it does provide a conceptual framework for understanding the emotions of dying. An understanding of these stages is important in counseling the patient and his family. It has even been found that when the stages of the patient and the survivors are synchronized, death is more peaceful and accepted more readily by all involved.

1. *Denial.* This is the patient's first response in order to cushion the impact of death. Death means the loss of everything on earth that matters to the patient. Denial helps him initially to cope with this prospect.

Denial surfaces in many threatening situations; so it is not surprising that it comes when death is close. Most psychoanalysts recognize that at the unconscious level people don't believe they will die. Thus when we are confronted with the prospect of death, it is very easy for us to hope by denying its reality.

Denial is also found among the family and hospital staff. Dr. Hans Mausch of the University of Missouri Medical School has found that health care professionals pass through the same stages their patients do.[2] Doctors, for example, see themselves as healers. A dying patient threatens that role. He and the patient may safely talk about the disease but do not readily touch on its fatal significance. In most cases, they will continue to talk about "safe" topics (i.e., current events, sports, fashion), which help to enforce the image of "business as usual."[3]

Although this is a very fragile pretense, it is not easily

broken. If either the patient or the hospital staff member is unwilling to talk, the silence will continue. The patient may send cues to the doctors or nurses that he or she wants to talk about dying, but unless they choose to respond, the silence will continue.

The difficulties are compounded when the family knows a patient is dying and keeps it a secret from him. Since most patients realize it when they are seriously ill, they see through this "make-believe" mask so that trust is further damaged. Surveys have shown that about four out of every five patients want to be told if they have an incurable disease.[4] Because of this, more doctors are now telling their patients their prognosis.

As a patient's health deteriorates, denial becomes a more difficult option to hold. The patient may find denial useful while he is trying to deal with death, but he needs to face reality so that he can begin putting things in order before he dies. In most cases this change takes place. Kubler-Ross reports that of five hundred patients she has studied, only four refused to the very last to admit they were dying.[5] But even they could at least talk about death.[6]

2. *Anger.* When a patient no longer denies his impending death, often feelings of anger and rage surface. This is often described as the "why me?" stage of dying. Anger is probably man's most frequent emotion against death. In a poem written to his aged father, Dylan Thomas gives this dubious advice, "Do not go gentle into that good night; rage, rage against the dying of the light."

In this stage, anger is vented in many ways—some of them in an unhealthy manner. Often the anger is released at whoever or whatever is handy. Doctors, nurses, and the family are frequent targets of anger. During this time, they should try to understand that the patient needs them, even if there appear to be few signs of need. Unfortunately, doctors, nurses, and family have a tendency to spend less time with the patient for fear of critical remarks.

In many cases, the target of abuse may be God. One should not be shocked by what is said. When our emotional nerve endings are raw, we often speak and think irrationally. Empathy rather than correction is probably the best therapy during the anger stage.

3. *Bargaining.* When anger subsides, bargaining usually begins. Just as a small child quickly learns that bargaining works better than angry demands, so a dying patient turns to bargaining. The question now shifts from "Why me?" to "Why now?" In an effort to have more time, the patient will often seek to bargain with the doctor, the family, or God in order to postpone the end. An offer of an exchange of good behavior for more time is often made.

During the bargaining stage, the medical personnel are also affected very subtly. Decisions need to be made concerning treatment. Special equipment and medication may be prescribed with the intent to perform a medical miracle rather than to relieve pain. When such a bargaining intent is on the mind of the doctor, it is difficult to exercise good clinical judgment concerning treatments that might hasten or postpone the inevitable.

The patient seeking a means of bargaining also may fail to exercise good judgment. He is very susceptible to entrepreneurs who are willing to strike medical bargains for large sums of money.

4. *Depression.* As a patient becomes fully cognizant of death, depression usually occurs. During this time the patient will be grieving for what he has already lost (i.e., health, mobility) and is about to lose (i.e., friends, family). Patients may mourn over the time they could have spent with their children or friends, the trip they will never take, or the loss of their future. It is commonly a period of silence and withdrawal

as the dying patient tries to separate himself from all he has known and loved. Kubler-Ross refers to this depression as "preparatory grief" because it allows a person to prepare for death by letting go of his attachments in life.

5. *Acceptance*. After this period of personal mourning, the patient realizes the end is near and is usually resigned to the situation. He has made peace with those around him, relinquished his unfulfilled dreams, and settled personal and financial affairs. The patient may once again enjoy the company of people, though many patients prefer to be alone. He no longer talks about the future but focuses on the tasks of everyday life before he dies.

Not all dying patients go through these five stages. Some stages may be skipped, and it is not uncommon for a patient to stay in a particular stage. Occasionally patients pass back and forth from one stage to another. When a patient and his family reach the acceptance stage, the process of grieving is usually shorter and less destructive. Accepting death does not mean that one does not care. It means that he cares enough to make the end of life as pleasant as possible for all concerned.

What Can I Do?

The best way you can help a dying person is to understand his situation and be compassionate toward him. Familiarity with these stages of dying is a good start. It can provide you with tools for counseling since an awareness of them can guide your expression of compassion and sympathy. As the figure on the following page shows, particular behavior on the part of the patient can elicit intelligent responses from family and friends.

The first thing you can do to help a dying person is develop a compassionate heart. Your desire to help should be tempered by a tender compassion for your friend. Without compassion and love, it is difficult to be a good counselor and

PATIENT REACTION	STAGE	FAMILY RESPONSE
The patient denies the possibility of death. He searches for a favorable diagnosis and denies the possibility of a poor prognosis.	DENIAL	Recognize that denial is a way in which a patient can begin to cope with his future. Be aware of nonverbal and verbal cues that he is willing to talk.
The patient says, "Why me?" He is angry with friends, family, God, or medical staff. He may be envious of good health and complain constantly.	ANGER	Be patient with him in his anger. Recognize he is losing every earthly thing and treat him with respect and compassion during this time when he needs human fellowship.
The patient says, "Why now?" Promises of good behavior are made in order to gain more time.	BARGAINING	Counsel the patient in his time of bargaining and recognize it as one of the stages of dying.
The patient grieves and mourns his approaching death. This is anticipatory grief.	DEPRESSION	Attempts to cheer the patient are usually not successful. Allow him to express sorrow fully.
The patient is neither angry nor depressed. He has accepted his impending death.	ACCEPTANCE	It is best to have close friends and family around the patient. It is not necessary or desirable to talk much.

Patient reaction and family response during the five stages of dying

comforter. When a loved one is facing death, it scares us and reminds us of our own death. Only love and compassion can conquer that fear. When a friend is angry and depressed, it is easier to stay away. Only love and compassion can give him the desire to do something he does not feel like doing. Therefore, it is important that we ask God to give us an understanding, tender, and compassionate heart.[7]

The second thing you must do is be honest. The channels of communication must be open, and they can stay open only if honesty is present. From the very beginning you should work to be a good communicator and comforter. This is often difficult since the first stage is usually initiated by the doctor's prognosis. In our desire to shield the patient from unpleasant feelings, we have a desire to keep information from him.

This is not good. Most patients want to be told if they are going to die, and it is unwise to keep such information from them. Dr. Herman Feifel of the University of Southern California Medical School says, "Ideally, the patient should be the first to know. The only question is how to tell the person. Some must be told gradually."[8] Only in rare cases may there be good reasons not to inform a person of his approaching death.

There are many reasons for letting the patient know. Most patients know they are going to die before they are told. Dr. Cicely Saunders of St. Christopher's Hospice in England has noted:

> In my own experience I find that the truth dawns gradually on many, even most, of the dying even when they do not ask and are not told. They accept it quietly and often gratefully but some may not wish to discuss it and we must respect their reticence.[9]

Dr. Elisabeth Kubler-Ross has also found that most of her patients knew they were terminal before the doctor told them.

Dr. Thomas Hackett, chief of psychiatric consultation services for Massachusetts General Hospital, who has pooled observations from many investigators,[10] confirms this observation. When patients are told the truth, they generally have fewer medical, emotional, and psychiatric complications.

If patients are not told the truth, they must suffer through hours of pointless, trivial talk when they often already suspect something is amiss. If told the truth, they can begin to put their earthly affairs in order. They will also feel less guilty about demanding services or attention if they and medical personnel both know the situation. Truth also gives the patient more freedom to express grief openly.

A third thing you can do is spend time with the dying. It is a natural reaction to turn away from death, but you must be willing to take time to listen and respond appropriately. We tend to treat the dying in the same way we treat the dead. For this reason, some researchers have referred to this avoidance phenomenon as the "bereavement of the dying."[11]

Why does this happen? There are probably many reasons. One reason is that we so anticipate our loss that we begin to deal with it *before* it occurs. We often try to cope with the anticipation of losing a friend by immediately severing ties.

Another reason we avoid the company of a dying friend is embarrassment. Many times we find it hard to go to a hospital to see our friend or loved one lying on a bed while we go naturally about our daily activities. Embarrassment soon leads to a feeling of guilt, and this feeling of guilt leads us to avoid the person who is dying.

Again, we sometimes develop an almost illogical anger toward the dying person because he is leaving us, and so we avoid him. Severing friendships is a painful process, and just because it is done by death does not blunt the anger that results from our feelings of desertion.

But regardless of the emotions we feel, we should strive to

be good comforters. The most important aspect of comfort is being a sensitive listener. Listening and responding appropriately are very important parts of becoming a good comforter and counselor.

When we respond, we should try to understand the situation. When a patient is expressing himself on an emotional level, he does not need logical arguments. He needs compassion and assurance on an emotional level. Conversely, when he is seeking advice about his personal affairs, he does not need emotional statements like "Don't worry, everything will be all right." He needs helpful advice about finances or other affairs.

In many cases good comfort may come from not saying a word. It may be hard to keep silent, but silence often speaks more eloquently than words. In other situations we may provide comfort by repeating, paraphrasing, or reinforcing some of the dying person's thoughts and feelings. Sometimes he may want to talk about his family, sometimes about sports or some other specific interest, and sometimes about his philosophy of life.

A fourth way you can help is to take time for prayer. When a dying person asks for prayer, you should be clear why you are praying. You should ask: (1) To whom are we praying? (2) For what are we going to pray? (3) How will we know what to pray? We should be praying to God according to His will. This may not mean that we are praying for a medical miracle. We often feel we should pray for a miracle when perhaps we should be praying for stamina and spiritual maturity for the dying patient.

Now let us look at some of the things that medical personnel can do for the dying. Let us consider the emotional and physical needs that they can meet so that the last days of the dying person will not be so traumatic.

What Can Be Done?

One of the greatest needs of the dying person is human companionship. He needs to know that those around him are deeply interested in him as a person. Family and friends can provide much of this need. But the medical staff should supplement this interest also. The family, in providing emotional support for the patient, will also need support.

It is good to know that there are many ways emotional support can be provided for the patient, family, and friends. Patients are often helped by concerned medical personnel. Doctors and nurses need to be willing to spend time with terminal patients and not simply write them off. Many nurses have special training in caring for terminal patients, and their comfort is readily welcomed by the patient.

In addition, in the last few years there have been many advances in health care that can aid the dying patient. The hospice concept, inspired by Dr. Cicely Saunders in England, provides a context in which dying patients can be treated for pain and other ailments while maintaining closer contact with loved ones.

The hospice program provides a coordinated program of doctors, nurses, and special consultants who help the dying person and his family through their time of struggle. Under hospice care, whether in a home or in a hospital, the medical staff seeks to eliminate a patient's fear of isolation while they pay special attention to the symptoms of the illness. This care is designed for terminal patients and differs from standard medical treatment in that it seeks to relieve the symptoms rather than cure the disease.

One of the most important emphases is the attempt to control and relieve chronic pain. Even minor discomfort, if extended for long periods, can have a debilitating effect. Medical personnel control pain by anticipating it and giving

27

analgesics and anxiety-reducing drugs.[12] In many cases narcotic drugs are used to deaden the pain. Many use "Brompton's mixture" or "Brompton's cocktail," made of morphine, cocaine, alcohol, syrup, and chloroform water. It dulls the patient's pain without dimming his alertness.

Hospices also provide support for the family. Having a person die at home is a much more traumatic event than ever before. Most of us are not prepared for such an event. About three out of every four people now die in a hospital bed. We have practiced a system of separateness in regard to the dying. But now the hospice team provides some of the emotional support the family needs by sharing the family's responsibilities. They take patients on outings and even help to prepare meals. These and other services help to relieve some of the strain a family feels.

Patients can be helped emotionally in other ways also. When there are psychological problems, there are many options open. For those problems that may have a physiological origin, there are forms of medication that will help relieve anxiety. When the anxiety is long-lasting and medication is needed, nurses may administer sedatives and tranquilizing drugs to reduce fear, agitation, and depression without making the patient particularly drowsy.[13]

When the anxiety is of psychological origin, counseling of various types is often available. In many cases, a friend's loving counsel will do a great deal of good. In others, professional help may be necessary.

When the anxiety is of a spiritual origin, a different kind of counseling should be used. Often the stress one feels about dying is due to the patient's uncertainty about life after death. Although more will be said about this in later chapters, the dying person needs to be counseled about his spiritual destiny. The Bible and many other books are available, as well as competent spiritual counsel from pastors and trained laymen.

Finally, emotional support to dying patients can be provided by groups. Many groups and organizations are devoted to the care of the terminally ill. One group called "Make Today Count" was founded by Orville Kelly, an Iowa newspaperman. It has a national network of over 159 chapters that help terminally ill patients through lectures and mutual support.

The dying patient also has many physical needs people can help meet. We have already seen the number of ways pain and anxiety can be combated through drugs. Many of those who push for aggressive forms of euthanasia today are misguided because they fail to appreciate the power of analgesics to control pain. Such pharmacological procedures virtually eliminate the scenario of a horrible, excruciating death. In most cases such drugs can eliminate pain without dulling the senses or shortening life.

In addition to giving pain-killing medication, medical personnel can do many things to relieve patient discomfort. An obstruction of the bowel can be by-passed surgically so that pain is diminished. Tumors can be removed from the throat or lungs to prevent distressing symptoms even though the cancer may continue to spread.

Patient discomfort can also be relieved by a variety of chemical means. In blood diseases, such as leukemia, the growth of abnormal blood cells can be slowed down, while transfusions enable the patient to participate in a fairly regular schedule of activities. Such palliative care procedures do not, in most cases, lengthen the life of the patient, but they do free him from a lot of pain.

Now let us look briefly at a very difficult problem in the area of dying—the death of children.

Dying Children

When children are dying of some terminal illness, it is difficult to really know what to do. It seems so outrageous that they are dying, and we feel helpless because we can do so little. Moreover, we often don't know what to tell them. Therefore most children with terminal illnesses are not told they are going to die.

While it is, of course, difficult to obtain direct information from dying children, some comments can be made about their reactions to dying. In each age group children show different reactions because of the different psychological orientation and understanding of death of the various age groups. The following is a summary of research on how children react to their own terminal illness, as presented by John E. Schowalter, Assistant Professor of Pediatrics and Psychiatry at the Yale University Child Study Center.[14]

Infants under the age of six months do not recognize that their environment is separate from them; thus death has little meaning. After the age of six months, a child's response to death is influenced primarily by those around him. Morbid grief reactions will cause great fear in the child and warp his view of life and death.

During their first three years, healthy children sometimes tend to resent parents because they are so dependent on them. On the other hand when a child is sick, he may be angry with his parents for failing to protect him. In some cases, when this anger is even greater than their fear of their illness, children may rebel against their parents.

The parent of a terminally ill child may react to this resentment in a variety of ways. He may feel guilt, grief, or anger. He may then dedicate himself exclusively to the care of the dying child, or else be so overcome by grief and so overwhelmed by the tragedy that he totally withdraws from the child.

Though there may be some harm to the family if both parents dedicate themselves totally to the dying child, even more harm can be done by neglect. It is the fear of separation, not the fear of dying, that haunts young children. It is crucial to their morale to have parental attention. We know how important it is for a non–fatally ill child to have parents near.[15] This nearness is even more important when the child is fatally ill.

Preschool children between the ages of three and five years first see death as something that happens to others. They still often do not understand its permanency; thus they respond with less anxiety to questions about death than children of other age groups.

Children at this age often see sickness as a punishment. Thus when they are dying they may feel a great deal of guilt. Children who appear passive as they are dying may have such a false sense of guilt. It is important that parents not neglect the feelings of the passive child but encourage him to express his feelings.

Some children become increasingly rebellious while they are in the hospital. This reaction often stems from their denial of their feelings of guilt and results in anger toward the medical staff and the family. Since a child often feels he is sick because of some failure on the part of the family or medical personnel, their retreat from his anger only confirms his feelings of not being adequately cared for. Though it may be hard, continued attention to the child will usually end his anger.

Death has a meaning of its own for early-school-aged children (ages 6 to 11). They are able to understand that death is a result of an external agent and not due to neglect or punishment. However, it is still not uncommon for children to continue feeling that sickness is a result of bad behavior. Yet because of their more sophisticated understanding of the causes of sickness and death, adults can help them understand that they are not the result of bad behavior.

Children in this age group often know they are dying and may ask if it is so. It is always best to answer these questions honestly, but not to answer them completely. Often a child merely wants to know why he is not feeling well and is content with a simple reason. If that is not sufficient, the parents may want to decide when and who should tell the child of his prognosis. In general, it is always best not to tell the child more than he asks.

When you tell a child he is going to die, His reactions are similar to those of other dying patients. Often he will deny the fact and then move through the various stages described earlier in this chapter. Clinical settings have verified that those children who deal with the news best are those who had earlier become aware of the reality of death in a nonfrightening way. Belief in God and a pleasant afterlife experience greatly lessens the fear of death.

A preadolescent or adolescent child usually has a nearly adult capacity to understand death. By the age of ten or eleven, he understand that death is universal and permanent. He will go through the same stages an adult goes through if he is told he is going to die.

There are some exceptions, though. This age group places more importance on physical features and autonomy. Treatment that causes the adolescent to lose his physical attractiveness and debilitating effects that cause him to lose control of his body can be devastating. Feelings of disgrace and lack of prestige can be destructive when the adolescent is beginning to establish an identity and a feeling of self-worth. Also, he may feel as if he has been cut off from life before he could achieve any lasting accomplishment.

Since members of this age group usually know they are dying, or at least are critically ill, it is probably best to share their prognosis with them, though there are many doctors who feel it is wrong to do so. Again, decisions should be made according to individual temperaments and situations. There is probably no one answer that is right in every instance.

In summary, the reaction of a dying person—whether a child, an adolescent, or an adult—to his impending death depends in large part on his understanding of death and on the attitudes of those around him. This reaction may vary from individual to individual and from age group to age group. Each situation must be faced with understanding and compassion.

In the next chapter we will shift our focus from dying to death. We will look at some of the types of responses to death that man has had both culturally and individually. Then we will look at grief and mourning in an effort to understand them and become good comforters. Finally, we will return to the question of children and see how death affects them and how they respond to grief.

THREE

DEALING
WITH
DEATH

How does a society deal with the universal fact—the inevitability—of death and how does it respond to the death of one or more of its members? What individual responses do people make to their own inevitable death and to the actual death of another? We will try to understand these responses in relation to studies that have been made of the process of grief and bereavement.

Cultural Responses to the Fact of Death

When people are confronted by a consideration of the inevitability of death, they may respond in a variety of ways. The contemplation of death is painful, frightening, and foreign. Let's first study some cultural responses to the fact of death.

In his book *Man's Concern With Death*, Arnold Toynbee devotes a section to "Traditional Attitudes Toward Death."[1] In it he describes various ways in which individuals have sought to reconcile themselves to the inescapability of death.

One response is hedonism. It is basically the philosophy of "eat, drink, and be merry for tomorrow we die." People seek to enjoy life as much as possible before death snatches it away. In its extreme form, hedonism is very destructive. Not only is it difficult to maintain for long periods (no one can perpetually enjoy himself), but it ultimately leads to chaos and total abandonment of morals. In the film *On the Beach,* Nevil Shute pictures Australians "living it up" as they face extermination by radiation from a previous nuclear war. Some sociologists today believe that immorality is a response to the impending threat of global annihilation.

A second response is pessimism. As early as the fifth century B.C., when the Greeks were at the height of their achievement in all fields of human endeavor, the Greek poet Sophocles declared that "it is best of all never to have been born, and second-best—second by far—if one has made his appearance in this world, to go back again, as quickly as may be, thither whence he has come."[2]

Modern despair is not very different. It, however, was born from the realization that, if nature is all there is, man is very insignificant. Naturalism does not enhance man's dignity or value. A naturalist does not see death as a door to another world. Death is simply a cruel wall. In his essay "Naturalism Reconsidered," Ernest Nagel states that "human destiny [is just] an episode between two oblivions."[3] Man is, in other words, a speck of intelligent consciousness surrounded by two eternities of nothingness.

A third response, especially by ancient man, is an attempt to deal with death by physical countermeasures. Ancient cultures assumed that life could be prolonged if the corpse was provided with food, drink, and other material goods. This reached the extreme with the building of the pyramids in ancient Egypt. The treasures we have found in the tomb of Tutankhamen indicate that they believed lavish countermeasures could insure immortality. In some cultures such provisions still exist today.

A fourth way man has sought to deal with death and over-come its devastation is by winning fame. In illiterate societies people often memorize genealogies and recite ancient wisdom. In literate societies written records are kept. Human beings have tried to insure their immortality through tombstone inscriptions, great books, and other forms of literature. In the age of the global village, the mass media produce a kind of immortality through fame.

But all of this is very unsatisfactory. True immortality cannot come from mortal work. As Woody Allen once put it, "I don't want to achieve immortality through my work. I want to achieve it through not dying."[4]

A fifth way people have sought to reconcile themselves to the fact of death is through future generations. They have sought to put their treasure in their successors. Future generations are a precious heritage. In Jewish history, for instance, one of the great promises God makes to the patriarch Abraham is that He will make him into a great nation (Genesis 12:2). But one's children cannot insure his personal immortality.

The four final ways of dealing with death as Toynbee lists them all deal with religious notions of immortality. Man has sought to obtain eternal life by (1) merging with the ultimate reality, (2) holding to the immortality of the soul, (3) believing in the resurrection of the body, and (4) having the hope of heaven and the fear of hell. We will deal with each of these notions in more detail in the final chapters of this book.

These ways in which people have made a cultural response to death are important because death is as much a social event as it is a personal one. Man is a social being and depends on other human beings both throughout life and in the final moments before death. He grows and develops in a community of persons who are interdependent.

When death comes, that interdependency is broken. As

John Macmurray said, "Death is at once our defeat at the hand of the forces of nature and our final isolation from the community of the living."[5]

Cultural Responses to the Occurrence of Death

Society must deal with the loss of a member in ways that are socially helpful and psychologically healthy. If it does not, the structures of the society, the strength of interpersonal relationships, and the psychological well-being of all may be disrupted.

Though cultural patterns may be important, realistic encounters with death are even more crucial. Kubler-Ross has noted that the earlier we are exposed to death, the easier our acceptance of the death of a loved one will be.[6] Unfortunately, in today's culture, we are rarely made aware of the reality of death while we are young. Robert Fulton, head of the Center for Death Education and Research at the University of Minnesota, has said that "this is the first death-free generation in the history of the world."[7] What he means is that the majority of people do not experience the death of another, and even if they do, they are rarely present when death occurs.

In a study of 560 bereaved persons, Fulton found that usually no family members were present at the deathbed. Most learned of death by a telephone call from a nurse, a secretary, or some other stranger.[8] Gone are the days when most people died at home in the presence of the family members. Today about three-fourths of all people die in an institutional setting like that of a hospital or a nursing home.[9]

But not only is death less visible, it is also further removed from our own sphere of existence. In 1900 two-thirds of the Americans who died were under the age of fifty. They were classmates, friends, close relatives. Today, most Americans are over the age of sixty-five when they die.[10] At that age they are much further removed from us. And, as we have already noted, they tend to be removed from us geographically as well as chronologically.

We must therefore work that much harder to deal effectively with death. Our cultural situation makes it harder, not easier, to deal with death. Many of the traditional family and institutional supports are gone, and the very presence of death itself has become a foreign item in our experience. Thus we must try to ensure that our individual responses to death are appropriate, beneficial, and healthy.

Individual Responses to Death

Because each of us has to face his own death, we reach a level of anxiety when we contemplate it. In order to cope with the daily affairs of life, we often seek ways to avoid thinking of death except in an impersonal way. These avoidance mechanisms may help us function in the world around us, but they also create barriers between us and others when death strikes a loved one.

One way we evade the personal implications of death is to see it as a generalized, public occurrence. In other words, we tend to see death as something that happens to people in general, not to anyone in particular. Traffic statistics, war casualties, or obituary columns rarely affect us. It is only when we know the person who has died or was killed that death takes on any personal meaning. It continues to be a generalized concept that is separate from real people and known situations.

A second way we avoid the personal nature of death is to see it only in a very oblique and abstract way. Death then loses its personal quality and assumes an unreal aura. Bodies in coffins no longer represent living persons. Our minds' distinctions and the mortician's makeup and preparation combine to erase the reality of death.

A third way we avoid death is to plan it out of our lives. It is said that only the old think of death. The rest plan vacations, business ventures, and other activities with no thought that these plans might be interrupted by death—either their own or that of others.

These, then, are a few ways in which we avoid the personal significance of death. We go about our daily activities with this death-denying view of the world. When death does come, we respond in a variety of ways that are related to ways we have tried to avoid it.

One of the most universal responses to death is *grief*. Though grief is closely identified with death, it should be noted that death is not the only event that brings feelings of grief to the surface. Almost any loss in our lives—loss of a job, the moving away of children or friends, etc.—will precipitate a measure of grief and a sense of loss.

In most cases grief is expressed in patterns similar to those of the grief of dying people. Although we will study these patterns in detail in the next section, it should be noted here that it is not at all uncommon for grief to produce anger or depression. It is as normal for some people to react this way as it is for others to express very little grief. Temperaments and situations differ, so it is hard to conceive of a "normative" response. Another response to death is often *feelings of guilt*. Those who grieve often feel very guilty about things they did by mistake or never carried out. Each of us wrongs others in this life, yet we can always say we are sorry if they are living. Death prevents us from apologizing to the one we have wronged.

However, though we cannot ask someone who has died to forgive us, we can ask God for forgiveness. It may be that we need to be forgiven for our actions. We often tend to treat the dead with more respect than we do the living. A grandmother whose family payed no attention to her while she lived may be dressed in the finest clothes at death. Those who were run off the road and killed are respected in death as every car gives way to a funeral procession.

But we may also feel guilty for no real reason. We may have done all we could for the one who has died. Death may have come in spite of our excellent care. In these situations we also need God and other people to comfort us.

Another reaction is *obligation*. Promises we have made to a person during his life often loom larger in death. Many people feel bound to spend their lives carrying out the wishes of the one who died. In such a situation it is best to remember that each of us has God-given abilities suited for our individual tasks. It may be very noble to live for another, but it may also cause us to neglect what is best for us.

Fear is another response each of us may exhibit when death comes. One of those surrounding Job called death the "king of terrors" (Job 18:14). Death is fearful and terrifying. To look into the face of death is to look into something evil and may cause us to be apprehensive about what lies beyond the curtain of death. Human beings have asked about the meaning of death century after century.

In summary, society has responded to death in many ways, as have individuals. Our cultural responses have ranged from hedonism to pessimism to hope for eternal life. Our individual responses have been grief, guilt, anger, obligation, and fear.

To understand our emotions and reactions to death, we will now look in more detail at the whole process of grief and bereavement.

Grief and Bereavement

We need to understand grief and how to work through it properly. Failure to do so can have disasterous consequences. For example, some children respond to the loss of a parent by becoming antisocial. One study of fourteen juvenile delinquents who were counseled in Los Angeles showed that they had all lost at least one parent through death.[11]

The same has been found for adults. When parents lose a child, the loss often puts a strain on the marriage. It is a well-known fact that divorce is a very common occurrence among couples who have lost a child.[12] We should therefore make sure that we understand the process of grief and how it affects us so we can help ourselves and counsel others in time of loss.

In 1944 Erich Lindemann published his classic study of grief, "Symptomatology and Management of Acute Grief." Though there have been many studies of grief since then, his still stands as the definitive study of the various stages of grief.[13]

The 101 patients he observed included (1) patients in the hospital who had lost a relative during treatment, (2) relatives of patients who had died in the hospital, (3) survivors of the 1943 Coconut Grove Fire, and (4) relatives of deceased members of the armed forces. From this diverse data base, he was able to understand the symptomatology of normal grief and to plot the course of normal, morbid, and anticipatory grief.

Since this study, others counseling in hospitals have also described the stages through which most patients and relatives pass. This is not to say that these stages are present in every case. Circumstances may alter the flow of emotional and other reactions. Differences in temperaments should always be taken into account whenever stages are described. Lindemann's study is helpful because it surveys the types of reactions people exhibit when grief strikes them.[14]

1. *The first stage of grief is shock.* In some people this shock may be very noticeable, but in others it may be latent. This variety of responses is similar to the reactions expressed by the dying patient. It is typical of people's response to any great loss.

Denial or shock has great value for a time because it helps the individual work through the feeling of loss without going to pieces. Often it is the only way some of us are able to cope with all the emotional and other details of a funeral service. When we attend a funeral and see such a person, we may comment on his great faith. We tend, inaccurately, to equate faith with a stoical attitude toward death.*

A good counselor knows that this stage is temporary. Someone might seem not to need help, and yet two or three days later wish someone would come to visit him. It is not unusual for shock to last for a few days, but if it goes on for several weeks, the individual should seek professional help. We should not be afraid of shock, however, as it is usually the first stage of a normal pattern of grief.

2. *The second stage of grief is usually the expression of strong emotions.* As the reality of the situation begins to strike home, strong emotions overwhelm us. This emotional release is very helpful and should not be shut up or it will be released in less healthy ways.

Men especially should not be so molded by cultural traditions concerning manliness that they bottle up their tears. Emotional release can be very therapeutic and is a natural way of releasing tension and pain. The Bible states that when great calamities came, great men of faith wept, often all night long. Nowhere in the Bible do we read that men are not to shed tears of pain or sorrow.

3. *In the third stage of grief, feelings of loneliness and depression are common.* By now, grief is in its full strength, and tears are probably the best therapy. It is also helpful to have others

---

*Some have felt that there is biblical support in such passages as 1 Thessalonians 4:13 for the notion that Christians are not to grieve. However, the context only notes that Christians should not grieve over the destiny of their loved ones the way those who have no hope do. The Bible is full of other references that show that grief is indeed proper, e.g., John 11:35.

around. Granted that no one has ever gone through another's specific experience, yet others have at least been through similar situations. They can be there to listen, provide insight, or put life in perspective.

In extreme situations, when grief is especially strong, it is not uncommon for feelings of suicide to surface. The terrible load of sadness seems too much to bear. It is best in such circumstances to have others around, or at least within calling distance, so that the one who grieves can receive compassionate, loving counsel.

It is also not uncommon for the man or woman of faith to harbor bad feelings against God. The loss of a loved one seems to cry out that God no longer cares and that His providence is ineffective or meaningless. It is good to remember at such times that other men of faith also shared these feelings. David cried, "How long, O LORD? Will you forget me forever? How long will you hide your face from me? How long must I wrestle with my thoughts and every day have sorrow in my heart?" (Ps. 13:1–2).

The best thing a friend can do at such a time is to reassure the bereaved with a quiet confidence that this depression will pass. Just as a cloud of fog clears, so will the feelings of depression. There *is* a light at the end of the tunnel! There is hope for the future. Depression is not a permanent state that will follow us the rest of our lives.

4. *Physical symptoms accompany emotional distress.* In some instances, the bereaved will manifest symptoms that parallel those that the deceased had shown after he became aware of his impending death. They are usually psychosomatic in origin and may manifest themselves for a variety of psychological reasons. It is not only medical personnel who should treat these symptoms. There should also be some counsel provided by psychiatrists, social workers, and pastors.

In other instances, these symptoms may only be minor

reactions to emotional distress. Grieving is often accompanied by a feeling of tightness in the throat, shortness of breath, or even choking. There is often a need to sigh in order to relax and relieve tension. Many complain of weariness and exhaustion during this time. Food loses its taste, and stomachs feel hollow. These are normal symptoms of grieving and will soon pass.

5. *Panic and fear are common emotions related to grief.* There comes a time when our constant thinking of the deceased begins to worry us. For a moment we might be distracted by something else, but then our mind returns to our grief. This causes us to begin to feel that something is mentally wrong with us. We panic because we cannot concentrate.

If we are prepared for this reaction, we will not panic so readily. When disturbing thoughts overwhelm us, our mind seems to play tricks on us. We begin to fear what we do not understand. It is comforting to know that even fear and panic are normal emotions related to grief.

In the opening entry in the diary he kept after his wife's death, C. S. Lewis noted:

> No one ever told me that grief felt so like fear. I am not afraid. The same fluttering in the stomach, the same restlessness, the yawning. I keep on swallowing.
>
> At other times it feels like being mildly drunk, or concussed. There is a sort of invisible blanket between the world and me. I find it hard to take in what anyone says. Or perhaps, hard to want to take it in. It is so uninteresting. Yet I want others to be about me. I dread the moments when the house is empty. If only they would talk to one another and not to me.[15]

Feelings of fear, restlessness, or apathy are not uncommon. They are not abnormal. They are a normal and predictable result of grief.

6. *Another symptom of grief is a feeling of guilt.* As we have already discussed, a feeling of guilt often arises out of our

inability to say we are sorry. Trips we planned but never took, visits we postponed, and arguments we never settled leave us with an overwhelming feeling of guilt.

We should be careful to distinguish between two different types of guilt. We feel guilty when we have done something or neglected to do something. That is normal. Neurotic guilt is feeling disproportionate guilt. Normal feelings of guilt can best be removed through prayer and assurance of the LORD's forgiveness. One who suffers neurotic guilt may need counseling. A person who feels guilty for not being with someone when he died, even though he could not be there, may need to talk to someone who understands the problem. If problems of this kind are not adequately dealt with soon, they may prevent further adjustment to the loss.

7. *Anger and hostility are common feelings during bereavement.* Often we may become angry or hostile because of the guilt we feel. We may get angry at ourselves or with members of the family, our friends, or the medical personnel. Such feelings are normal. What is more, even the most devout person may feel angry with God, even though he may try to suppress it. In ancient times people felt freer to express their anger toward God. But today we see few who beat their breast, tear their clothing or wail because of their sorrows.

When such anger is expressed, those surrounding the bereaved should not be shocked by the powerful emotions that surface. These emotions do not reflect careful intellectual consideration; they are the raw emotions one feels in the moment of loss.

A poignant example of this can be found in the book *A Grief Observed,* in which C. S. Lewis plumbs the depths of his despair and anger. Anyone familiar with his writing is usually shocked at the emotions he feels at the death of his wife. Here one of the most prominent apologists for the Christian faith is bitterly angry toward God! Later in the book Lewis himself expresses shock at what he wrote as he reflects back on his initial feelings.

It was probably this shock that led him to publish the book initially under a pseudonymn. Even the man who had answered many of the philosophical problems of evil, pain, and death in his book *The Problem of Pain* was not exempt from the painful emotions and irrational thought that accompany grief. Neither are we.

8. *There is resistance to performing usual activities.* It often seems like an outrage to resume daily activities too soon as if nothing happened. It is much more tempting to cancel all major engagements.

In many circumstances, it is not that we do not want to reenter normal activities. Rather, we find it difficult, even impossible to do so. Something seems to hold us back. This is because our society makes it so difficult for us to return to normal living. Grief may last for quite some time and be full of strong emotion. Our societal norms do not make any adjustment for people to be "out of commission" for lengthy periods because of grief, nor does it allow open expressions of grief. We find it impossible to reenter normal life because we have not adequately traveled through the various stages of grief.

Friends and counselors should be careful not to abandon the person closest to the deceased as soon as the funeral is over. Once it is over, family members and out-of-town visitors leave and the true grief begins. This is an important time to contact the bereaved and offer to help. Bringing meals, doing dishes, or just being there are important and often forgotten ways to help the bereaved individual return to normal.

At the time of loss, of course, the individual needs immediate help. But even then we should allow that person to make some decisions. It is not a good idea to take over all the activities in the home (cooking, cleaning, babysitting). The bereaved person should still make some decisions, even though a feeling of listlessness may persist as a result of the emotional stress of mourning.

Moving toward the later stages of grief, the bereaved individual should be encouraged to assume larger tasks. We should make sure that we relinquish our control of these tasks to allow for a resumption of a daily routine.

9. *One of the final stages of grief is hope.* After a time the clouds begin to part and hope for the future begins to return. We begin to establish new relationships and put our lives in order once again. In many ways these new relationships may be of a different character than previous ones, but they are a part of life. As Joshua Liebman says in his chapter on grief:

> The melody that the loved one played upon the piano of your life will never be played quite that way again, but we must not close the keyboard and allow the instrument to gather dust. We must seek out other artists of the spirit, new friends who gradually will help us to find the road to life again, who will walk that road with us.[16]

10. *The final stage is a struggle to affirm reality.* As the bereaved resumes his usual patterns, he must establish a new position in life. He is not the same person he was before. He has assumed new roles and has new facets to his personality.

The degree of struggle needed to reach this stage varies. For those with a mature faith and good psychological preparation the struggle may not be very great. For others it may be much more difficult. Those who are prepared are like the athlete who is trained and ready to compete. Others are often caught unaware. They need more time to sort things out.

These are the ten stages of grief we may experience when we lose a person close to us. We move from shock and denial to acceptance and affirmation. If we undergo this struggle, we emerge as healthy, renewed members of society.

Let us now consider how we can help those who mourn.

Mourning

In our society, outward expressions of emotion have normally been frowned upon, though this attitude is changing. During periods of mourning, however, people feel and express sympathy for those who mourn. During times of grief it is important that others be with the bereaved in order to provide help and comfort and emotional release.

But we need to do more than just want to help and comfort. We should know something about how to comfort. Job was surrounded by those who wanted to help him in his time of need, but he called them all "miserable comforters" (Job 16:2). In order to be good comforters we must learn how to comfort.

A foremost need is to feel tender and compassionate toward those who mourn. Just as we need to be compassionate toward the dying, we need to feel compassion for the mourner. This compassion should help us discern what each situation requires. We might need to encourage some people and join them in the fellowship of weeping. To help others, we may need simply to listen as the bereaved person shares his sorrow. For still others, we may be required to take over the daily activities of the household in an effort to bring some sense of order out of a chaotic situation. Only a sincere interest and compassion can help us discern the true needs of others during this very difficult time.

A second need—already mentioned—is that we be willing to listen. The Bible states that "he who holds his tongue is wise" (Prov. 10:19) and admonishes us to be "quick to listen, slow to speak" (James 1:19). In times of grief, an economy of words is often most helpful.

Death is an especially uncomfortable experience, so we must work very hard not to succumb to the desire to break its uncomfortable silences of mourning. But it is nevertheless usually best to listen and not speak. Sensitivity to the situation is crucial and should make us *more* silent and *more* willing to listen.

Joe Bayly tells of two people who came to visit him when he was in grief over the loss of one of his sons. One spoke many obvious truths that he already knew and was never quiet. Joe could hardly wait for the man to leave. Another came, was quiet, listened, and had a time of prayer. He was sorry to see this friend leave.[17] Silence can be so very much more important than words in time of grief.

Third, when we do talk, it is often best not to make death or the deceased a taboo topic. Often in our compassion for others we assume that even mentioning the name of the deceased will reopen the floodgates of grief.

While mentioning the deceased's name may bring tears, it is also true that many who mourn don't want to forget their loved one. Even a year later, some people feel uneasy about mentioning the deceased in casual conversation. While we might desire not to open a new wound, the survivor may long for some indication that the deceased is still remembered by his friends.

Fourth, we should help the mourner through the stages of grief by providing constant and consistent concern. One of the most disconcerting things about grief is that because of it, it is easy for one to lose balance and perspective in life. The process of grief usually does not follow the neat ten-step formula previously outlined. New circumstances and fresh outpourings of grief affect the process of healing. We should be sensitive to changing emotional needs.

When C. S. Lewis had passed through many of the stages of grief, he noted in his journal that he seemed to be regressing.

> Tonight all the hells of young grief have opened again; the mad words, the bitter resentment, the fluttering in the stomach, the

nightmare unreality, the wallowed-in tears. For in grief nothing "stays put." One keeps on emerging from a phase, but it always recurs. Round and round. Everything repeats. Am I going in circles, or dare I hope I am on a spiral?[18]

For some the clouds roll away quickly, but for others it is a more painful process. One event may trigger a flood of emotions. Only a community of concerned persons can be an adequate support to lean on.

Fifth, encourage those who mourn to express their inner feelings. Our present cultural context does not often allow those with difficulties to express them. Sharing thoughts, emotions, and memories allows them to get rid of their pain in a healthy manner.

In many cases, writing can be a good vehicle for the venting of grief. C. S. Lewis poured out his feelings of grief in journals that later became his book *A Grief Observed.* One minister who counsels those who are mourning encourages them to write down all the ways everyday life has changed since their loss.[19] Such modes of expression aid the processes that eventually bring about healing.

Sixth, encourage the bereaved individual to read. Those who grieve are comforted to learn that their experiences are not unique. Books like *A Grief Observed* by C. S. Lewis, *The View From a Hearse* by Joe Bayly, *A Severe Mercy* by Sheldon Vanauken, or *Where Is God When It Hurts?* by Philip Yancey are good for them to read. * Knowing that others have traveled the path before and have adjusted to their new circumstances provides great comfort.

Finally, provide spiritual comfort. When death strikes, our thoughts are immediately turned to questions of the afterlife as well as the questions about our own strength to endure the pain. Use the Bible to answer the mourner's questions. We

---

*See "For Further Reading," p. 195, for more details about these books.

need to minister not only to the individual's emotional needs but to his spiritual needs as well.

Prayer is also a vital ingredient. Praying with the grief-stricken individual develops a strong bond of fellowship with him and places your perspective on a proper spiritual plane. In her article "How Not to be a Miserable Comforter," Majorie Brumme tells of a heartbroken mother's comments about the value of prayer to her.[20] She appreciated those who prayed with her and could not understand Christians who would give her advice but would not offer to pray.

These, then, are seven ways to help those who mourn. Society also helps to assuage a mourner's grief by funeral ceremonies and other customs of mourning.

These customs have a place. They are not useless vestiges of the past but genuine helps for those who are grieving. In his book *Dying*, John Hinton adds that

> The practice of mourning provides more than this socially approved catharsis of grief. It insists that the death has occurred, repeatedly demonstrating this fact in various ways over a few days so that the bereaved, whatever their state of mind, accept the painful knowledge, assimilate it and can begin to plan accordingly.[21]

The recent practice of skipping funeral ceremonies is unwise. Viewing the body and taking part in the funeral services often helps people make important psychological adjustments. These activities do not reflect a morbid fascination with death. They affirm a loss and further the healing process of grief.

The funeral also serves to bring the community together to mourn the passing of one of its members. This social function honors the dead and provides condolences for the survivors. And after the funeral, people share memories as they eat and drink in a lighter vein.

In a time of decreasing formality, the funeral provides an outlet for healthy mourning. Visits to the household are no longer required by rules of etiquette. Widows rarely dress in black and widowers seldom wear black armbands. Gone are the formal rituals that marked mourning in the Victorian era. The funeral is the last social custom by which an individual can express his sorrow openly.

Funerals also serve to reemphasize a person's worth and value at a time when he does not seem worthy of much respect. They provide one of society's affirmations that people are of greater value than other forms of life. Toynbee wrote:

> At different times and places the dead bodies of human beings have been honored in an amazing variety of ways. They have been buried in graves or in tombs or under tumli or inside pyramids. They have been burnt on pyres, and the ashes have been preserved in urns or have been scattered to the winds. But however diverse man's funerary rites have been, they have all had a common signification. They have signified that a human being has dignity in virtue of his being human; that his dignity survives his death; and that therefore his dead body must not simply be treated as garbage and be thrown away like the carcass of a dead non-human creature, or like a human being's worn-out boots or clothes.[22]

It is lamentable that there is so very little in our society that upholds those in mourning. The funeral service is the last vestige of ancient practices of mourning. Aside from the lamentable fact that it is on the wane, it is too short. Dr. Herman Feifel, a clinical psychologist at the University of Southern California, says, "My studies show that grief lasts a minimum of about two years, yet our funeral rites last only a week or a month at most."[23] Something needs to be done to help those who mourn.

In summary, there are certain things we can do as individuals for those who mourn. Many of the social contexts through which people express their grief are significant.

Let us turn now to the very difficult subject of death and

children to understand the distinctive attitude of children toward death and grief.

Death and Children

The questions children ask about death are not answered any more easily than those dying children ask. The major difference is that the questions are not quite as agonizing. The problem is how to explain death in such a way that it is still meaningful but not frightening.

As in many other parent-child situations, the attitude of the parent is of foremost importance. If the parents weep when they are confronted by grief, the child learns that death means hurt and disappointment. If grief leads to uncontrolled hysteria, a child's attitude toward life and death may be seriously distorted.

But probably in most cases neither of these possibilities surfaces. Rather, it has been common for many parents to treat death the way they treat sex—they refuse to discuss it. Soon a child realizes that it is a taboo subject and stops asking questions about it. Or, as Professor Wallace Denton of Purdue's Marriage and Family Counseling Center points out:

> Some children never say anything or show signs of grief. It may be that in some way a child has decided that he can't talk about death. Parents in this situation may initiate the subject and indicate that he can talk about it.[24]

Often it is only when parents talk about death that a child begins to show signs of grief. Until then, he may continue to deny the reality of death.

This leads to two important questions. First, when do you tell a child about death? At what age is he able to understand and deal with the concept of death? Second, how do you tell him about death? How do you describe it so he will understand? Let's take a look at these questions.

Death education should begin as soon as a child develops meaningful speech and can distinguish between animate and inanimate objects. By the time he is two, a child can be helped to understand that tables and chairs are not alive, and dogs and cats are.[25]

If this is done early enough, children can integrate concepts of death with other concepts they are acquiring about the world. If the explanation comes much later when fantasies are lively and aggressive thoughts are more pronounced, they may be incorporated with aggressive fantasies and be harder to assimilate.

If this initial education is begun early, children will later develop realistic concepts of death. A study of four hundred school children showed that those under the age of five years did not recognize death as final. They saw it more like sleep or departure. Life and death were not recognized as mutually exclusive so that phrases like "very badly killed" might be used.[26]

A study of English children also indicated that by the age of seven or eight they had a considerable understanding of death. They began associating death with such things as burial, killing, lying horizontal, and hospital treatment. They had a good sense of what it meant biologically to die.[27]

Against this background of an intellectual understanding of death, children can begin to understand death in terms of loss by about the age of four. At that age and older, a child can be helped to master the loss of a friend or relative.[28] At this age it is wise to explain death to children when it enters their lives.

How should we tell children about death? What should we say? The answers to these questions will vary according to age, maturity, and situation, but here are a few guidelines.

It is important to tell children about death in terms they can understand. If a pet dies, an object lesson about death can be given. But the use of simple language and concepts should not mean the sacrifice of accuracy. If we say that the deceased has gone away, we must make sure that the child knows that this is permanent and not just for a period of time.

It is also wise not to compare death with sleep. If you tell the child that his mother went to sleep and will rest peacefully forever, that will probably terrify the child. The next time he is thinking about what you said and is told to go to sleep, he may break down in tears. Sleep will then be feared, not welcomed.

Sensitivity is also important in phrasing religious explanations. If a religious explanation is used in a family that has no religious background it will probably mean little and could result in a negative view of religion. In families with religious backgrounds, adverse reactions could result if explanations are not phrased carefully. Telling a child that someone died because Jesus loved him so much He took him can backfire. The next Sunday he may hear that Jesus loves him very much and fear that he too will die in a very short time.

Religious explanations, however, are very good ways to communicate the meaning of death to the child. A Christian view of death, heaven, and the nature of man as described in later chapters in this book are good ways to give a child true concepts about death. If death is linked to a description of heaven as a happy place, there will be few tears and little sadness at the death of a relative or friend.

Even when death has been properly communicated and our attitudes are right, there may nevertheless be times when a child will respond in an unusual way to death. Let us look at the causes of such responses so we can understand why they surface.

Sometimes children exhibit a morbid fear of death because of a psychological problem they may have. If they feel unworthy, they may become preoccupied with thoughts about death. When a child is very close to a friend, he may be afraid that friend will die and the friendship will end.

It is not uncommon for children to fear that their parents (particularly their mothers) may die because they are so dependent on them. Or they may feel guilty about their relationship with a parent or bewildered by the uncertainty of their world. For whatever reason, children may have a fear of death.

When someone close to a child dies (a brother, sister, or parent), make sure he knows he was not the cause. If a brother or sister dies, he should know that it was not due to some evil wish or a feeling of rivalry. A child who was angry with a parent before the parent died may feel that he caused the parent's death and may need to be reassured that it was not his fault.

Such feelings can further manifest themselves in the form of denial. The following case history provided by Robert Furman, Director of the Cleveland Center for Research in Child Development, illustrates this point:

> Four months after his mother had died, the patient's denial was first noted when he took, from his teacher, two tickets rather than one ticket for a PTA meeting. He did this though he was aware that the teacher knew of his recent loss. In addition, in his psychoanalytic sessions he wanted to walk to an adjacent hillock a few blocks away where his mother had sometimes parked while waiting for his session to end. In exploring this behavior it emerged that he feared his anger had made his mother angry and that this anger had caused her death. After this was discussed his denial stopped. Whenever it recurred, we found that he had again become convinced that he was in some way responsible for her death. It also recurred when he experienced anger toward her for having died and left him.[30]

Thus we see that many of the stages adults go through in grief are also manifested in children. The significant difference is that children sometimes draw erroneous conclusions that prevent them from moving through those stages.

When a child loses a parent, many of the activities that

were done with that parent exclusively cause extreme pain. Shopping, getting haircuts, going to baseball games, etc., may all lose their appeal because they are so closely tied to the child's sense of loss. It becomes the difficult task of the surviving parent to recognize these activities and work to replace them. In many cases these activities represent needs, and until children (especially young children) feel they will be met, they will not be free to deal with their feelings. Once the need for food, clothing, protection, and certain other needs are filled, children may successfully deal with their feelings of grief.

Preparing a child for the loss of a parent is also very difficult. In many cases it is impossible. When death is sudden, there is no time to prepare the child. If the child, for example, witnessed the accident that killed his mother, it is particularly important for him to be given a repeated opportunity to express his feelings.[31]

In a case in which death is impending, some preparation can be made. It is not reasonable to expect a child to recognize it and cope with it. When the care of a child can be transferred to a successor while the parent is still alive, it is most effective. But it may be too difficult for a parent to entrust his child's need for care and affection to another person in his last days.[32]

Parents often wonder if their children should attend funerals. Children as young as seven can take part in a family's mourning. You must ask yourself whether the child is capable of participating along with the other adults and older children in the family. If so, the next question is whether the child wishes to participate.

Children should not be forced to attend a funeral. Studies have shown that many are terrified by funerals, especially if it involves seeing or touching a corpse.[33] Though it is beneficial for children to attend a funeral service, if they do not wish to do so it is wise to leave them behind.

If a child attends a funeral, some arrangements should

probably be changed. First, it may be wise not to have an open casket. Second, there should not be lines of people being greeted at the funeral. These two provisions should work to eliminate some of the potentially harmful effects a funeral may have.[34]

In summary, our attitudes about death and grief are important. We should tell children about death in a clear but honest way, beginning as early as two years of age. Finally, children for a variety of reasons sometimes have adverse reactions toward death.

How does a person adjust to life after death takes a loved one? The adjustment period after death is a very difficult time and we need to understand it clearly.

Adjustment and Restoration

When a household loses a loved one, the pieces are often not easy to put back together in a meaningful way. The usual patterns of the household are interrupted, and everyone feels some disorientation. The family must begin the process of establishing new identities and creating new patterns.

When the loss takes place within the family unit (as opposed to the loss of, say, a second cousin or a grandparent), it can be extremely painful. The small family units ("nuclear families") of our society feel such a loss intensely, much more so than in "extended families" as in former days or in other cultures. The likelihood of finding a substitute for the one who has died is very small, since the relationships with the deceased were unique. Living in small family units creates very close and complex relationships between each of the members.

Because of the social catastrophe a death causes in a household, modern man must attempt to develop some form of restoration. New relationships must be established so that the remaining family members, especially the children, can resume the normal patterns of life.

When a parent has been lost, it is especially crucial that the household remain structured. A child needs to feel that there will still be some continuity in his life. Radical changes in structure should be avoided.

Familiar structures can be maintained in a number of ways. First, make sure that there is someone of the opposite sex present to provide a balanced male-female model for the child. In some cases this may require hiring a housekeeper if you are a father who must work during the day. In other cases, a grandparent might be able to join your home. Close married friends with children may also be able to offer some after-school supervision.

Second, maintain discipline. Do not change previously established standards and guidelines, even though you may feel wrong about imposing them on a grieving child. If children learn that grief excuses bad behavior, they may use it as a crutch the rest of their lives and never thoroughly work through their own grief.

In some cases, it may be wise to let older children take over some of the household responsibilities. But though they may become partners in the work, they should not be treated as peers. Many specialists see this "instant-adult treatment" as a mistake made by many widowed parents.[35]

Third, maintain the memory of the deceased. Pictures of the deceased parent with the child can remind them of the relationship they once had. Remembering the parent's birthdays and the anniversary of his death is also important. Do not overemphasize the memory of the deceased, but at the same time make sure his significance in the child's life is not forgotten by neglect.[36]

When a child dies, a different set of options are available. Sometimes if the parents are young, they may want to have another child. But they must be careful not to "replace" the former child. Parents often give the new infant the same name as that of the departed child and expect it to mature in a similar way. Such behavior is unlikely to help the newborn child in any way and may scar him psychologically.

Having additional children is not wrong, of course. But parents must make sure they examine their motives. Planning to have another child to compensate for their grief is unwise. Not only may such a purpose affect the newborn, it may prevent the healing of their own grief.

Couples who have older children but want to have another should consider adopting a child or caring for a foster child. Or they may consider getting involved in local children's groups (Boy Scouts, Girl Scouts, YMCA, YWCA, PTA, etc.). Spending with other children time that you might have spent with the one you lost is a beneficial and generous gift to others in the community.

You may also seek ways to help others who have lost loved ones. Those suffering bereavement appreciate a truly sympathetic ear. There are numerous groups that offer such an avenue of service.

It is particularly important that we help widows. They face many adjustment problems. Our society places a premium on the matrimonial bond, and a widow who knows she is not likely to find anyone to replace her deceased husband is often left out of community activities and fellowship. She faces much the same problems as the divorcee, including both grief and social stigma.[37]

The Bible admonishes the church to take care of widows (1 Tim. 5:3–16), but the church in our society does very little for most widows. In other cultures the widow is often taken by some man as an additional wife to give her a place in the community. While such an arrangement may be wrong, the concept is worthy of note. Members of society should seek to provide a niche in their lives for the widow.

Sometimes widows and widowers remarry. Studies have

shown that such a marriage requires adjustments that take time to work through properly. Comparisons with the past should be avoided and ties with old friends and relatives should often be loosened. When children are involved, difficulties are usually solved with affection and in time.[38]

Dating after the death of a spouse can cause another set of problems. Dr. Herman Feifel warns, "First of all, don't date to get over your grief. Once you start dating, it should be the signal that you have worked the mourning through."[39] To catch someone "on the rebound" to overcome grief is a common mistake that can lead to a very shaky relationship.

Do not remarry hastily for your children's sake. To do so is to impose unnatural burdens on children and grownups alike. Children's reactions to the parent's dating and remarriage are often mixed. A child may want another parent but he may have trouble accepting a different man or woman in that role. Even if he overcomes that hurdle, there are other adjustments when a new person's lifestyle has to be incorporated into the family's existing patterns. Keep the channels of communication with your children open and anticipate potential difficulties.

In summary, there are many problems associated with grief. There cultural and personal reactions as one goes through the stages of grief at a time of loss. When children experience grief, there are some peculiar and occasionally abnormal responses that can be resolved with patience and understanding. Finally, there are some basic principles that help bring about a final resolution and an adjustment to the world.

We now turn our focus to the questions associated with death and the world beyond it. What about the afterlife? In our discussions about dying and death the constant theme of hope appears. Not only do we talk about the temporary hope of recovery or restoration, but we talk of the ultimate hope of life after death. We want to know where the dying are going, if anywhere. We want to know where our loved ones who have died are now. These are issues we will deal with in the following chapters.

FOUR

LIFE
AND
AFTERLIFE

In what is perhaps the best-known of Shakespeare's plays, Hamlet ponders the question of life. Even though he is convinced that life is not worth living, he decides to continue living because he fears the world on the other side. He is unwilling to set out for "the undiscover'd country, from whose bourn/ No traveller returns," and says that our ignorance of what lies beyond "makes us rather bear those ills we have/ Than fly to others that we know not of."[1]

As it was for Hamlet, so it is for us. We do not know much about that undiscovered country of death. We do not know where we will go when we die. We do not know what we will find when we arrive.

Destination Unknown

It is perhaps the ultimate irony of the twentieth century that we know so much about this life and this world but so little about the afterlife and the afterworld. People have vastly increased their fabulous store of knowledge about the world with the aid of microscopes, telescopes, and other sophisto-cated instruments but they have never invented a device to penetrate the curtain of death. The world beyond is still a mystery.

In previous ages people conceived of death as a door into another world. They lived in a culture in which it was not uncommon to see death, and so they lived with one eye on the afterlife. This view was not a morbid one but an outgrowth of the religious and philosophical perspective of the day. Their philosophy of death conditioned their actions in life.

Philosophers have long noted that the relationship between death and a person's philosophy is very strong. Socrates and Karl Jaspers, though separated by two millennia, have both held that the essence of philosophy is preparation for death. In the past most people were not terrified by death but prepared for it and saw it as a transition to a new and better life.

Often this view was an outgrowth of their faith in God. They believed they would have eternal life and looked forward to an existence after death. Others held a view of agnostic optimism. Socrates, for example, did not fear death, since

> to fear death is nothing other than to think oneself wise when one is not; for it is to think one knows what one does not know. No man knows whether death may not even turn out to be the greatest of blessings for a human being; and yet people fear it as if they knew for certain that it is the greatest of evils.[2]

The fear of death, however, is natural. Bacon said, "Men fear death as children fear the dark." But in our present age of naturalism and materialism, man is even more anxious about death, because he sees it as extinction. If matter is all there is, death is not a door but a concrete wall. Death is not just the end of life; it is the end of everything. As the philosopher Bertrand Russell put it, "There is darkness without, and when I die there will be darkness within. There is no splendour, no vastness anywhere; only triviality for a moment, and then nothing."[3] Many of our leading thinkers see their lives as short interludes of biological activity surrounded by two eternities of nothingness.

Such a view has led to a crisis in values. We have seen that the death of the idea of God and an afterlife has ultimately led to the loss of man's significance. It is difficult for us to attribute meaning and dignity and value to human beings if they are destined for ultimate extinction. Death creates a crisis in values. As the eminent psychologist Carl Jung noted, "The question of the meaning and worth of life never becomes more urgent or more agonizing than when we see the final breath leave the body which a moment before was living."[4]

In an effort to find some meaning in life, twentieth-century man has looked at religious and scientific advances. The growth of many of the modern religious movements is a result of man's desire to find some meaning apart from traditional religious answers. But such a search has been disappointing. In the midst of controversies concerning solicitation and brainwashing, few have found any meaning.

Others have turned to the Eastern religions. Most promise immortality by merging one's consciousness with the absolute oneness of the universe. But though it might preserve one's consciousness, there is no promise that one may preserve one's individual identity. There is little value in becoming another drop in a galactic ocean of consciousness if individual identity is lost.

Still others have looked for hope and meaning in scientific thought. Astronomers search the universe for signs of life, and many hope that other companions in space will give us some answers. Biologists study the effects of aging, and many long for a scientific breakthrough that will enable human beings to be immortal. Presently, though, it seems only a vague hope that man may discover meaning or immortality. Science can offer only what many of the religions of the world seem to offer—a hope of immortality.

If all we can do is hope for immortality, how will we ever know if there is life after death? We may want to believe in life beyond the grave, but it may be a false hope. We may long for eternal life, but it may be only an unattainable desire. If the twentieth-century view of man and the world is correct, Bertrand Russell is right when he says that "no fire, no heroism, no intensity of thought and feeling, can preserve an individual life beyond the grave."[5]

Grave New World

Is the grave the final place for man? The books on the shelves of most bookstores say no. There is an abundance of books that claim there is a world *beyond* the grave. Many of these books base their claims on the messages received by mediums in seances. Yet, even though these have been around for some time, they have never attracted much attention. But now there is another category of books that base their claims on the dying and near-death experiences of thousands of people.

Much of the initial work in this field came from those involved in research of psychic phenomena. One of the first studies came from the Parapsychology Foundation. Dr. Karlis Osis wrote a monograph on *Deathbed Observations by Physicians and Nurses* in order to collect material on the experiences of dying patients systematically. He later joined with Dr. Erlendur Haraldsson to write the book *At the Hour of Death,* which compared the cultures of the United States and India on the subject of death.

Other books on the subject soon appeared. Archie Matson wrote *Afterlife,* and Scott Rogo wrote *Man Does Survive Death,* both citing the deathbed experiences of patients and various other psychic phenomena suggestive of survival after death.

Although many of these books appeared in bookstores, none of them gained the prominence achieved by the book *Life*

After Life by Dr. Raymond Moody. Initially published by Mockingbird Books, it was picked up by Bantam Books and became a bestseller. Despite its acclaim, it was a bit of an anomaly when published. Most of the other scientific books on death were written by those involved in psychic research, whereas Moody had degrees in philosophy and was pursuing a medical degree. Most of the other books cited numerous historical cases of afterlife experiences or deathbed reports; Dr. Moody reported only the experiences of those who had clinically died and were resuscitated. At the time of the publication of his book, he was apparently unaware of the vast literature on psychic research into the afterlife.

This fresh perspective coupled with a popular writing style and anecdotes made the book a bestseller. A sequel, *Reflections on Life After Life*, soon followed. Soon sections of his first book appeared in *Reader's Digest*, newsmagazines, newspapers, and *Guideposts*. For the first time in ages studies on the afterlife were being eagerly sought by the general public.

The popularity of this book led to a veritable avalanche of books on the subject of life after death. Titles such as *The Evidence for Life After Death, The Case for Immortality*, and *Journey to the Other Side* stocked the nation's bookshelves. They dangled before an eager public the hope that man will exist after physical death. They claimed that there were people who had been behind death's curtain and returned for an encore. What these people saw convinced them that none of life's actors need fear the final curtain.

Death's Curtain Drawn

The central case for life after death in these books is based on the experiences of those who had a close brush with death. Moody's study, for example, was based on interviews with about 150 people who either had a close encounter with death (i.e., were in an accident) or were actually clinically dead (i.e., had an absence of clinically detectable vital signs). From these 150 people, Moody selected fifty first-hand testimonies.

Unlike other authors, Moody chose to lump his testimonies together into a composite experience. This composite experience contains many of the common elements of many of the testimonies that were reported to him. However, not every element in the composite is found in each experience. In fact, no one reported *all* the elements contained in his composite picture.

Moody describes a man on an operating table who heard the doctor pronounce him dead. He then heard a loud, buzzing sound in his head and felt himself being moved down a long dark tunnel. Suddenly he found he was outside his own body; so he could watch like a spectator. Soon he saw the spirits of relatives and friends who had already died. He then encountered a "being of light" who showed him an instant review of his past life and deeds. Finally he learned that his time to die had not yet come and he was returned to his physical body.[6]

Upon returning to their bodies, people find it difficult to communicate their experiences. First, they cannot find words to describe the experience, since it seems to transcend finite, three-dimensional words. Second, they often encounter skepticism from friends and medical personnel. Many of the testimonies gathered by Moody are from patients who, hearing of the reports of others, broke long years of silence to recount their own past near-death encounters.

Limitations in the Research

Before we critically assess these reports that come from behind the curtain of death, it is important to recognize certain limitations. *First, there are no outside, objective observers of these events.* We are limited to the subjective experiences of people whose identity is kept anonymous. The significant material is often lost in a maze of anecdotes of the kind that tend to fill every book on the subject. Many of the testimonies cannot be read in context, because there has been a selective grid used to filter material for publication. Even when the selection of material is not a problem, there is no way to retrace the steps of the researchers. Not only is the patient's identity kept anonymous, but we are given little or no information concerning his medical, psychiatric, or personal history.*

Second, these experiences cannot be confirmed scientifically. One of the fundamental tenets of the scientific method is repeatability. None of these experiences has been repeated. Moreover, they are outside of other forms of verification. Any experience we have should always be evaluated in light of further experiment. Our senses are limited and fallible. Information that is accepted solely on the basis of personal experience is much less authoritative than information that comes from rigorous scientific experiment.

Third, we are limited by the language of the testimonies. We have only the reports of these experiences, which were private (except in the case of deathbed reports like those found in *At the Hour of Death*). That means we must rely solely on the memory and reporting of the patient. Such reporting is very crude and allows for the possibility of embellishment and suppression in reporting. The problem is compounded by the fact that the language is vague. Many express frustration in trying to communicate what took place because their experience defies language.

Fourth, we are often limited by the very means of reporting these experiences. Since the publication of Moody's book, there has been a general tendency to restrict all discussion to the composite experience. This is unwise because it does not take into

---

*I am not arguing that a patient's confidentiality be violated but merely noting one problem that plagues any researcher attempting to use these books as source material for evaluation.

account different and divergent elements of the near-death encounter. Those features that do not "fit" the preconceived pattern have a greater tendency to be overlooked in light of the "normal" elements. It is also unwise because it tends to channel discussion along a prescribed line so that it deals only with the generalized description and not with specific events. Researchers have often sought to analyze these testimonies in terms of the death of the patient.

This is not necessary. Many of the patients who reported elements of the composite experience did not die clinically (one of the conditions of the composite experience). The elements they reported took place completely apart from any encounter with death. One example is the reported review of a subject's life. While it is true that some people report this as a feature of their near-death encounter, it is also experienced by those in non–life-threatening situations. But since it is listed as an element of the composite experience, most researchers have felt the need to explain it as a paranormal phenomenon of death.

The composite experience also tends to define all future experiences in terms of a norm. It is often seen as the complete or normative experience and all other experiences are judged by it. In actual fact, no two experiences completely concur in every detail. Each differs from others at some point. But it is even more disturbing that no one in Moody's original sample reported all the elements of the composite experience.

The composite experience also tends to artificially "order" these experiences. There is no consistent order of events in the testimonies. In one case the review phenomenon precedes the out-of-body experience; in other cases it succeeds it. More often the reports are a confusing set of subjective experiences. It is often very difficult to tell where facts leave off and interpretation begins. There is much less agreement in detail and in sequence than the composite experience implies. The only way these divergent reports can be harmonized is to assume that the differences encountered were due to interpretations individuals placed on a common experience.

Therefore rather than addressing the composite experience, we will look at a few of the individual elements. We will look at some of the reports that have come from those who were clinically dead and were resuscitated and from those who reported their experiences to others on their deathbeds. Before we begin this analysis, we must clarify two issues. First, are these experiences merely hallucinations or visions of a sick brain? Are they illusions or are they reality? Second, were the people who had the visions of the afterlife really dead or were they in some twilight stage that precedes death?

Illusion or Reality?

Many people in the medical profession tend to pass these visions off as simply clinical phenomena. They ascribe them to some form of hallucination brought on by loss of oxygen or a drug reaction. They assume that they have some physiological, psychological, or pharmacological explanation.

In many cases (perhaps most) such explanations are correct. As we shall see in the next chapter, there is good reason to believe that a percentage of what is reported does have normal, natural explanations. But there are experiences we might call paranormal that apparently defy the normal, medical explanations often put forth.

These visions may be due to some *physiological* action. Although it might be tempting to explain these visions as the product of a sick or defective brain, there is evidence to the contrary. A sick brain produces fewer visions than a clear one. Dr. Karlis Osis found that "the clearer the patient's mind, the more strong this experience was. So it looks like it is not the result of a sick brain. There was something existential happening."[7]

There may be *psychological* or *pharmacological* explanations for these phenomena. Initially when Dr. Elisabeth Kubler-Ross confronted the patients who reported visions after clinical death, she assumed they had been hallucinating. While she was in the room with them they would often appear to be conversing with spirits she could not see. In some cases they probably were hallucinating. Some of her elderly patients were either psychotic or heavily drugged. The problem is that many of them were neither and yet had the same kind of visions. Often they would appear quite coherent in their conversations with Kubler-Ross and did not manifest any symptoms of hallucination while having these visions.[8]

Patients who have experienced hallucinations in the past also report that their near-death experiences were very different. In *Life After Life* one patient reported that

> it was nothing like a hallucination. I have had hallucinations once, when I was given codine in the hospital. But that had happened long before the accident which really killed me. And this experience was nothing like the hallucinations. Nothing like them at all.[9]

In his book *Return From Tomorrow,* Dr. George G. Richie reports that he found little in common between his study of fantasy and hallucination in his field of psychiatry and his own afterlife experience.[10] It seems unlikely, therefore, that many of the visions people reported are due to some form of hallucination. The visions they report are usually too coherent to be hallucinatory. Patients who had a medical history that might produce hallucinations did indeed have hallucinations that were rambling, disjointed, and concerned with "this-world purposes."[11] Patients whose brains were impaired by high fever or disease reported fewer visions than those who were alert. In fact, powerful drugs such as morphine and Demerol actually decreased the coherence of the visions.[12] In contrast, we find that most of the experiences reported by those who had an encounter with death were remarkably logical and coherent.

Dead or Dying?

The next question we should try to answer is whether these people were really dead. Those on their deathbeds who reported what they were seeing obviously were not dead. But what about those who claimed to have died and returned? Were they really dead or were they dying?

The answer is not simple. Death may be an event or it may be a process, as Robert Morison has noted:

> Most discussions of death and dying shift uneasily, and often more or less unconsciously, from one point of view to another. On the one hand, the common noun "death" is thought of as standing for a clearly defined event. A step function that puts a sharp end to life. On the other, dying is seen as a long-drawn-out process that begins when life itself begins and is not completed in any given organism until the last cell ceases to convert energy.[13]

Most medical personnel will acknowledge that death is a process more than an event. It is often described as a series of irreversible changes that take place in various organs of the body at different times. There is no sharply defined end. The standard legal definition of death is "the cessation of life, the ceasing to exist defined by physicians as a total stoppage of the circulation of the blood, and a cessation of the animal and vital functions consequent thereupon, such as respiration, pulsation, etc."[14]

Definitions like this, however, have become unsatisfactory. With the advent of cardio-pulmonary resuscitation (CPR), it is possible to keep people alive even though spontaneous heartbeat and respiration have ceased. To say that these people are dead is a distortion of the facts.

For example, it is known that man can voluntarily stop his heart or lungs for a period of time without ill effects. Many textbooks on physiology cite Colonel Townsend who deliberately stopped breathing for so long that a panel of doctors in London certified that he was dead and went home. It is also known that many swamis in India have such control of their hearts that they can stop them for a long as twelve minutes.[15] It is possible that they might be declared legally dead even though we know they are very much alive!

It is not uncommon for people to have more than one heart stoppage without ill effects. In Moscow, for example, a woman's heart stopped and started twenty-four times within a two-day period.[16] To announce that she died and came back to life twenty-four times would be extreme. There are even instances of people who have had heart stoppages over ninety times.[17] To state that they had "died" more than ninety times would severely tax any definition of death.

If the heart and lungs are poor indicators of death, we should look elsewhere to pinpoint the moment of death. Many medical persons have suggested that lack of brain waves be selected as the determinant of death. Brain activity can be measured by an electroencephalograph (EEG) so that a flat EEG pattern should be an indication that the brain has irrevocably ceased to function. Many biologists suggest that a flat EEG for a few minutes is sufficient to determine that any meaningful life is extinct, though there are some who adhere to a twenty-four- or forty-eight-hour time limit.

There are some difficulties with this method. It is often difficult to administer and there are occasions when flat readings may be obtained from those who are not dead (i.e., those suffering from severe barbiturate poisoning or from hypothermia).[18] But recognizing these limitations, an ad hoc committee of Harvard University physicians, theologians, lawyers, and philosophers established guidelines for new criteria for determining death. When the criteria are satisfied, there is almost complete certainty that the patient is dead.

This definition may seem overly restrictive, but we should remember that a correct diagnosis of death is absolutely crucial. In Shakespeare's *Romeo and Juliet,* Romeo comes upon the comatose body of Juliet. He makes a hasty diagnosis of the drug-induced suspended animation provided by Friar Laurence, and a beautiful love story becomes a terrible tragedy. Modern doctors, utilizing an imperfect definition of death, have often made the same mistake.

A thirty-eight-year-old woman who had been pronounced dead shocked coroners in California when she gasped for breath in the county morgue while a deputy was shifting her body from one table to another.[19] In a class in which I was speaking on the topic of euthanasia, one student shared a story of a man who revived in the mortuary, got up, and went home, thereby leaving the funeral director with an inaccurate death certificate.

One of the most dramatic examples of misdiagnosis took place in Chu Lai, Vietnam, in 1967 when Jacky Bayne's police dog stepped on a land mine and Jacky had to be rushed to a field hospital. When he arrived, physicians could find no pulse, breathing, or audible heartbeat. After working for forty-five minutes, they still found no signs of life. The doctors, the electrocardiograph, and the electroencephalograph all said he was dead.

After he lay on a table in Graves Registration for four hours, an embalmer began the cutdown on the groin in order to inject embalming fluid. To his surprise, his corpse had a pulse! He quickly dispatched Bayne's body to the hospital, and he was brought back to consciousness. Although he suffered some brain damage, he is alive and is living today in Illinois.[20]

Given such mistakes, it is even more important to ask whether the people who had these afterlife experiences were really dead. Dr. Moody deals with this subject in some detail.

He lists the following definitions of death: (1) the absence of clinically detectable vital signs, (2) the absence of brain-wave activity, and (3) the irreversible loss of vital functions.

How do Moody's people fit into these three catagories? First, there are those who didn't even come close to death. They reported a crisis situation in which some of the elements of the composite took place. Their experiences do not conform to any of the definitions of death. Second, some of the cases may fit under the first definition of death. There is no way to know if any would be classified under the second definition since the reported cases involved emergency situations in which it was impossible to set up an EEG. Moody states that none of the cases he cites would qualify under the third definition.[21]

Since none of these reports came from people who were conclusively over death's brink, Moody is careful to refer to these accounts as near-death experiences. Even though a patient may have heard himself pronounced dead, we must be careful to keep from making claims that go beyond the data. Psychiatrist Richard Blacher says, "The trouble lies in the subtle extrapolation that these experiences occurred after dying. Death is not the same as dying. Flying to San Francisco is not the same as being in San Francisco. Just because the patient heard the doctor say she was dead doesn't mean she was dead."[22]

These people were not dead but dying. It is also possible that much of what they experienced took place *before* they entered what we should call the near-death experience. A vision that occurred before vital signs ceased could have been later interpreted as part of the death experience.

In summary, there are a number of reports of the afterlife that have come from those who were judged clinically dead but who had not actually died or from those who were present with dying patients. These reports appear to indicate that the people who had near-death encounters were not simply hallucinating.

In the next chapter we will endeavor to explore some of the features of these near-death experiences and offer explanations for them.

FIVE

AN ANALYSIS
OF THESE
EXPERIENCES

The deathbed visions and afterlife experiences reported in many books are remarkable in their claims. But it is important that a careful analysis be made before they are accepted as authentic. We need to look at some of the physiological, psychological, and pharmacological explanations that have been postulated for many of the elements in these experiences.

The Curtain of Death

In many of the afterlife experiences that have been reported, patients describe being enveloped in darkness. This darkness may be described as a dark room or a long, dark tunnel. In either case it is as if during the first few moments of death the person is surrounded by a dark, quiet curtain.

The explanation for this phenomenon appears to be strictly physiological. Lack of oxygen in the brain (cerebral anoxia) seems to be responsible in most cases for these experiences. Dr. Marshall Goldberg, who has interviewed many patients resuscitated from cardiac arrest, reports that

> after cessation of the heart, it still takes three or four minutes for the brain to die, and certain patients—if interviewed before a

81

> rapidly developing amnesia effaces the memory—can relate what
> the experience is like. For some, it is surprisingly peaceful, as if a
> soundproof, pain-deadening curtain has descended over them. . . .
> I now have heard similar descriptions from enough patients to
> accept it almost as the predictable result of terminal oxygen lack.[1]

Based on these types of medical experiences, it seems that cerebral anoxia is primarily responsible for the curtain of death that many describe on their deathbeds or upon returning from a near-death encounter. It also appears that a lack of oxygen can trigger other phenomena. One physician told of two experiences that could be connected to a lack of oxygen and resulted in visual imagery:

> One was a drowning experience which triggered off such beautiful
> imagery that he was unhappy at being rescued and revived. The
> other occurred when he was flying at a high altitude and his oxy-
> gen supply became frozen—again beautiful color visions oc-
> curred.[2]

On the whole, however, few of the elements can be explained solely on the basis of physiological phenomena. Others involve different phenomena. But there is good reason to believe that the curtain of death and some visual imagery are physiologically caused.

Review for the Final Exam

The life-review phenomenon is a good example of features that are reported in death and afterlife situations as well as in non–life-threatening situations. In some cases, people report that this review is initiated by a being of light as one of the first experiences, while most others report that it occurs at other times in the afterlife sequence.

Since this phenomenon occurs in situations that are not associated with death, we might suspect that it is triggered by something other than death. This is probably the case. Many people report "flashbacks." Often this may be a reflection on a previous event brought to memory by a single sight, sound, or smell. After a time of sudden stress or danger, people will report that their "whole life" passed before them.

What is this experience like? Many describe it as a rapid review of the major points in their lives. It is often very vivid, realistic, and filled with imagery. Some describe sounds and smells as well as visual images. In some cases there is a temporal sequence to the review, but not always. Some patients report that the flashbacks began with their early childhood and progressed sequentially.[3] Others report that they began with the most recent events and regressed to the most remote.[4]

Most of those who describe the review say it is more like an educational review than a time of judgment. One person described it as an "autobiographical slide-show."[5] In the situations in which the review is correlated with contact with a being of light, the review becomes part of a conversation. The questions that the being raises do not accuse or threaten, but are more like Socratic questions that help the individual proceed along a path to truth.[6]

If this is what it is like, how is it brought about? In this case, psychological stresses trigger some physiological events. Stress is often sufficient to trigger the review phenomenon. This is the explanation for reviews of the past in non–life-threatening situations.

In many cases, stress brought on by grief can trigger the life review. Those who are dying, those who feel some grief, and grief-striken survivors often experience a review of their lives. Especially during acute stages of grief, a bereaved person may report memories of deceased people.[7] Noyes and Kletti report an example of a panoramic memory that was reported by a young woman three days after the death of her husband:

> I began to see, in bright colors, a review of the outstanding events that occurred in our lives together. It was like a three-dimensional color movie without sound. Each scene lasted only seconds but, as in a dream, they seemed to last hours, days, weeks, I do not know how long. Time had no meaning although the events I pictured were progressive. . . . The last one began with the illness of my husband and ended with his death.[8]

In other instances the review can be brought on by stress on the body's physiology from a fearful encounter. One man related an accident he had while driving a truck. He had a very rapid review of his life as the truck skidded across the road. All of this took place in a few seconds and was precipitated by stress alone since he didn't even receive a scratch in the accident.[9]

A mountaineer described a similar experience. As he was falling, he saw his possible fate, the results for those left behind, and countless pictures of his past life. All of this took place in the five to ten seconds he was falling before he hit the ground.[10]

Physiologically, the life review is probably related to heightened arousal and temporal lobe function.[11] Under stress or grief, the hypothalamus in the brain will signal the pituitary to secrete a hormone (ACTH), and this arousal appears to be sufficient to initiate a life review. Since arousal involves the limbic system, which is in close proximity to the spinal cord and cerebral hemispheres, it is not surprising that there is often a recall not only of visual images but of emotions and smells as well.

It has been well known for some time that a vivid review of past events can be initiated artificially by placing a probe on a patricular location of the brain surface. Operations on epileptic patients to locate damaged tissue often produce such reviews of the patients' lives. As an electrode is moved over the surface of the brain, patients describe specific scenes from the past. These are often reenacted with such detail that sights, sounds, and in some cases odors are vividly reported.[12]

If these come from memory recall of past events, how are they arranged in such coherent patterns? This arrangement seems to be a natural function of the mind. Various sensory association areas in our brain are capable of orchestrating isolated bits of information into coherent patterns.

A good example of this can be found in the book *The Road of Xanadu* by John Livingston Lowes. Lowes carefully analyzes the poem "Kubla Kahn" by Samuel Taylor Coleridge and shows that virtually every word and phrase in the poem stems from some item in Coleridge's past reading or experience. What is most interesting is that Coleridge noted that the poem came to him, line after line, in a dream. The explanation lies in the mind's ability to place these sensations and thoughts into a coherent pattern. Unhampered by external stimuli, the sensory association areas of the brain coordinated the lines of the poem.[13] In the very same way it is possible for the mind to put together an autobiographical life review from isolated past experiences stored in the brain.

In conclusion, the life-review phenomenon occurs in situations apart from clinical death, and there are reasonable physiological and psychological explanations for it. Though it is possible that there is a connection between these deathbed and near-death experiences, there is no compelling reason for interconnecting the two, since life reviews also occur totally apart from life-threatening situations.

Out-of-Body Experiences

In most near-death encounters people describe a stage in which they come out of their bodies. Though their physical body may lie on the bed, there is another part of them that leaves the physical body and is able to look down on the scene. They are having an out-of-body experience (OBE).

Many report that their OBE appears to take place in another dimension of reality. Normal laws of nature often do not appear to function in their experience. Their attempts to communicate with the living are always futile since no one can hear them, and their attempts to touch others fail because their out-of-body hands produce no physical effects.

There appear to be two consciousnesses operating during these experiences. In an address to the Royal Medical Society in Edinburgh, the late Lord Geddes described it as follows:

> By 10 o'clock I had developed all the symptoms of very acute poisoning . . . pulse and respirations being quite impossible to count. I realized I was very ill and very quickly reviewed my whole financial position . . . thereafter at no time did my consciousness appear to be in any way dimmed, but suddenly I realised that *my* consciousness was separating from another consciousness which was also me. These for the purposes of description we could call the A and B consciousnesses, and throughout what follows the ego attached itself to the A consciousness. The B personality I recognized as belonging to the body, and as my physical conditions grew worse . . . I realised that was beginning to show signs of being composite, that is, built up of "consciousness" from the head, heart, viscera, etc. The components became more individual and the B consciousness began to disintegrate, while the A consciousness, which was now me, seemed to be altogether outside the body, which it could see. Gradually I realized that I could see not only my body and the bed in which it was, but everything in the whole house and garden, and then I realised that I was not only seeing "things" at home, but in London and in Scotland, in fact wherever my attention was directed it seemed to me; and the explanation I received, from what source I do not know, but which I found myself calling my mentor, was that I was free in a time dimension of space, wherein "now" was in some way equivalent to "here" in the ordinary three dimensional world, but also "things" in these four and more dimensional places that I was in.[14]

Before we begin to look at possible explanations for these out-of-body experiences, we should note that they are not a new phenomenon. Many books on the subject give the erroneous impression that OBEs have begun only recently. That is simply not true. Plato in *The Republic* describes the OBE of Er, a Greek soldier, for example. He saw his own body about to be burned on a funeral pyre and realized he was out of his physical body. After having further afterlife experiences, he awoke on the pyre and reported his experiences to Plato.[15]

Plutarch, writing about A.D. 79, tells the story of Aridaeus, a soldier from Asia Minor, who became unconscious after a severe fall. When he recovered he told of being conscious during that time and talking to dead kinsmen who told him he was not really dead because he was still "made fast to the body." He eventually returned to his physical body and described the process "like suddenly being sucked through a tube."[16]

One of the earliest detailed scientific reports was made by Dr. Wiltse in the November 1889 issue of the *St. Louis Medical and Surgical Journal*. After falling into a coma, he lost all signs of life (heartbeat, respiration) and was pronounced dead by Dr. S. H. Raynes. Upon returning to life he noted that his nonphysical body resembled that of a jellyfish and that he was in another dimension. His body passed through those of others in the room without contact, and any attempts he made to communicate with them failed.[17]

Since 1889 there have been many reports made of out-of-body experiences. A number of these reports have come from people who have not had a near-death encounter. As we will see later, there are whole religious movements dedicated to producing spontaneous OBEs and scientific establishments that are studying these experiences. Therefore we should not view these out-of-body experiences as something recent or merely associated with a brush with death. They are well known and there are explanations for them.

First, let us look at some of the physiological explanations for OBEs. As with the review phenomenon, stress can be a factor that will initiate an out-of-body experience. A mountaineer described an OBE that was precipitated by his fall over the edge of a ridge. He explains his experience before the moment his fall was arrested by his rope. He felt a rush of power come over him that reached a crescendo.

> Then suddenly this feeling was superceded by a feeling of complete indifference and detachment as to what was happening or likely to happen to that body. I seemed to stand aside from my body. I was not falling for the reason that I was not in a dimension where it was possible to fall. I, that is, my consciousness, was apart from my body and not in the least concerned with what was befalling it.[18]

There are, therefore, explanations for OBEs apart from a near-death encounter that involves clinical death.

There are other possible explanations for OBEs. Most of the explanations that have been proposed would only explain a few of the many that have been recorded. For example, it is possible that cerebral anoxia (oxygen shortage to brain) may have caused some OBEs. It is known that a limited supply of oxygen or an excess of carbon dioxide sometimes produces abnormal mental states.[19] But it is unlikely that either of these factors can account for many of the OBE reports, since the effects are different and many of the OBEs occurred before any significant oxygen lack occurred.[20]

It is also known that fever can sometimes trigger an OBE. In her book *Out-of-the-Body Experiences* Celia Green notes the relationship between fever and OBEs: "As my temperature was getting higher and higher I became aware that I was no longer in my body but up in the corner of my cubicle watching the nurses flitting about . . . bathing the body lying in my bed, etc."[21] However, fever may explain only a few of these cases. In most of the cases reported there were no major physiological causes that could be listed as factors contributing to OBEs.

Since there is a residual amount of brain activity even

during these near-death encounters, it is possible that some of the OBEs can be explained on the basis of some psychological reaction. In the midst of some emergency or threat, the brain may respond reflexively by an OBE as a protective device.[22] Sigmund Freud held this view. He said that we tend to remove death from our consciousness by becoming detached observers, since "our own death is indeed unimaginable and whenever we make the attempt to imagine it, we can perceive that we really survive as spectators."[23]

More recently Russell Noyes and Roy Kletti have argued that depersonalization is the nearly universal reaction to life-threatening danger; thus OBEs may be some form of psychological phenomenon.[24] A good case can be made for such a conclusion since many OBEs involve a cluster of events associated with depersonalization (feeling of unreality, sense of detachment, panoramic memory). It is quite possible that many of these OBEs are merely projections by the brain to help a person cope with the approach of death.

There are also pharmacological explanations for some OBEs. In most cases drugs were not responsible for the experiences patients report, but there are some that should be mentioned. It is interesting to note that drugs are used by some primitive tribes to elicit OBEs during their religious ceremonies.[25] In modern societies, there are many drugs that also produce such effects. Alcohol can sometimes produce an OBE. Charles Tart has reported that 44 percent of marijuana users experience an OBE.[26]

When LSD was discovered by accident in 1943 one of the first effects reported was its tendency to produce OBEs. Dr. Albert Hofmann reported:

> I lost all control of time: space and time became more and more disorganized and I was overcome with fears that I was going crazy. The worst part of it was that I was clearly aware of my condition though I was incapable of stopping it. Occasionally I felt

89

as being outside of my body. I thought I had died. My "ego" was
suspended somewhere in space and I saw my body lying dead on
the sofa. I observed and registered clearly that my "alter ego" was
moving around the room moaning.[27]

Since that time, it has been well documented that leaving
one's own body is a frequent occurrence in psychedelic sessions involving LSD.[28]

It has also been found that certain anesthetics can produce
out-of-body effects. About 10 to 15 percent of patients emerging from ketamine anesthesia show hallucinatory reactions
of some kind,[29] and patients who are given nitrous oxide
(laughing gas) have reported having an OBE.[30] It is remarkable how closely ketamine reactions simulate many near-
death encounters. On one occasion a person reported, "I'm
moving through some kind of train tunnel. There are all sorts
of lights and colors, mostly in the center, far, far away, far
away, and little people and stuff running around the walks of
the tube, like little cartoon nebbishes, they're pretty close."[31]
People on other drugs report other features that those who
have had a near-death encounter have also reported—review
of their lives, visions of other beings, etc. Obviously there are
differences, but we must be careful to eliminate those features
that can be explained by normal phenomena before consider-
ing paranormal claims.

But even when we do find physiological, psychological,
and pharmacological explanations for many of the reported
OBEs, we must admit that some have no normal explanation.
There are those that must be described as paranormal. One
reason is that there are features of many OBEs that tax any
natural explanation. Information that could not be gathered
in a normal way is gathered by the patient during his OBE.

For example, those who experience near-death encounters
routinely report a heightened sensory awareness. They are
able to hear and see more vividly. The colors and sounds they

report are too incredible to describe. A rather dramatic example can be seen in the report of a research chemist. Although he had been blinded a year earlier in a laboratory accident, he was able to see during his OBE and could accurately report everything that took place during his near-death encounter.[32]

It is not unusual for patients to be able to report to a doctor later what took place while they were clinically dead. What they are able to report is accurate in detail and related with great precision. It is amazing that they had any conscious memory of the event at all, yet they report details with remarkable accuracy (including events which took place outside the room where their body lay).

This, along with other data, seems to confirm the notion that OBEs are not hallucinations but true experiences initiated by a variety of phenomena. Dr. Stuart Tremlow, a psychiatrist involved in transpersonal psychology (ESP, biofeedback, OBEs), has shown that OBEs can be induced in the laboratory by drugs, hypnotic suggestion, or electrical stimulation of the brain (ESB). This is a description of his first induced journey out of the body.

> I experienced the separation of my mind from my body. In this state I sped down a long, dark tunnel, and found myself back in Topeka. I saw my wife go out to the kitchen for a drink of water and then return to the couch in the living room. I drew close to her for a few moments and then moved to a mirror to find out if I could see any reflection. I could not. Then I moved on.
>
> I said nothing of this to my wife, who is skeptical about such matters. But without prodding she told me that one night while I was in Kentucky she got up to get a drink in the kitchen and then settled down to sleep on the living-room couch. She said while she was lying there she felt a shadow come close to her and then move toward the mirror.[33]

Tremlow is not the only one studying this phenomenon. At the Stanford Research Institute, Drs. Harold Puthoff and Russell Targ have been studying the OBEs of Ingo Swann.

Since he was a little child, Swann has been having out-of-the-body experiences.

At the Institute these doctors have been studying the phenomenon of "remote viewing." Swann would lie down and be asked to describe targets placed on a platform out of sight. His task was to "float up out of his body" and observe the objects. Then he was to sketch the objects. When the series of experiments were complete, the targets and the drawings were submitted to an independent judge who correctly matched each copy with its original.[34]

Swann later topped off his out-of-the-body career with an out-of-this-world experience. Nine months before NASA's Pioneer 10 spacecraft was scheduled to bypass Jupiter, Ingo Swann and Harold Sherman made an out-of-body trip to the planet. On April 27, 1973, Sherman left from Arkansas, and Swann left from California. Dr. Harold Puthoff and Russell Targ recorded the data. Although separated by nearly 2,300 miles, both described a planetary environment of ice crystals, high-velocity winds, great mountain ranges, and powerful magnetic fields, all of which were later found by Pioneer 10.[35]

Nearly a year later, a similar experiment was undertaken to the planet Mercury. Despite the prevailing theory that Mercury would not have an atmosphere or a magnetic field, both insisted otherwise. Nineteen days later, on 29 Match 1974, data from Mariner 10 showed both conditions.[36]

The existence of genuine OBEs has not only been verified by experiments, it has also been validated by numerous experiences. Many people are learning how to induce OBEs. Probably the best known teacher for OBEs is Robert Monroe, author of *Journeys Out of the Body*. His program M-5000, located in Afton, Virginia (with branch programs in other cities, including San Francisco), teaches people how to get out of their bodies.

The weekend training course costs $175 (besides meals

and motel room) and consists of listening to a series of forty-five-minute tapes that use a combination of sounds and instructions to generate an OBE. Though not everyone gets out of his body on the first try, it is claimed that with practice everyone can have an OBE. Of the hundreds of people who have tried the program, one of the more illustrious people to experience an OBE was Dr. Elisabeth Kubler-Ross. She got out of her body both times she took the program.

Robert Monroe discovered his ability to get out of his body in a rather unusual way. While sleeping one night, he suddenly discovered himself floating twelve feet above the floor. As he looked down, he noticed that his wife was in bed with someone he thought was another man.

> Assuming himself to be dreaming, Monroe studied the male form curiously. "Just who would I dream to be in bed with my wife?" he pondered. Then, peering more closely, Monroe says he recognized the man as himself. "I must be dead!" was his terrified reaction. Desperately he swooped down to his body and dove in. Then, feeling the bed below and the covers above, he cautiously opened his eyes and saw the room from a more familiar perspective.[37]

After this adventurous beginning, Monroe discovered he could leave his body at will and began to develop the system of audio pulsing tapes that enables others to do so.

Monroe, however, was not the first to document out-of-body experiences. In fact, his book was written years after many of the other significant books on the subject.[38]

In addition to this research, there are many religious movements that have experimented with out-of-body experiences. Paul Twitchell brought the cult Eckankar to the United States and taught his followers "the ancient art of soul travel." Today under the leadership of Sri Darwin Gross, the group enjoys a sizable following that seeks higher levels of consciousness through OBEs.

In the East there are religious movements that also use

OBEs. Paramahansa Yogananda in his book *Autobiography of a Yoga* speaks of getting out of his body. He tells of having 360° vision during his OBE, and he even encounters his old guru Sri Yukesteswar returning from beyond the curtain of death. He notes that the very touch of his old guru was like that of human flesh.[39]

In conclusion, there may be some normal phenomena that trigger an OBE, but there appears to be good evidence that most of these experiences are paranormal. In other words, we cannot explain them in terms of normal brain-body interactions. There is something more—the immaterial part of man. We are dealing with more than just a body. We are dealing with a whole person, in whom body and soul are united. Possibly during times of OBEs there is a kind of separation between the two entities. At that juncture there is apparently a split between the spiritual and the physical aspects of the person.

In chapter 6 we will look at this phenomenon in greater detail after we have looked more closely at the nature of man. But for now it is important to note that even if OBEs do exist (as they seem to), they tell us very little of the afterlife. The OBEs may tell us a great deal about the nature of man, but they tell us little about the nature of life after death. The fact that man may have an immaterial nature does not in any way establish that he has an immortal one.

An example of this error in reasoning can be seen in the interest in using OBEs as therapy for dying patients. Monroe's Star Program attempts to give terminally ill patients an OBE so that they may be prepared for the afterlife. The program, which has advisors like Kubler-Ross, offers a "trial run" for the actual experience. According to Monroe, "If there is a great beyond, there's a place for out-of-body. Given three months, we can easily train a person to achieve out-of-body experience and change his concept of death and establish a beachhead where he's going."[40]

Some have even gone so far as to suggest that OBEs be used to eliminate the fear of death. These people say that OBEs could help terminally ill patients and those in high-risk vocations. According to John Palmer:

> Many persons who have had striking OBEs report that the experience convinced them of survival after death and eliminated their fear of death. Whether or not this conclusion is objectively valid, it does suggest therapeutic possibilities for the OBE. . . . (It) may help persons engaged in high-risk occupations . . . where fear . . . may adversely affect . . . performance. (It) might also provide comfort to patients in certain stages of terminal illness.[41]

Despite the great hope, nothing of the sort can be undertaken. Just because a person is able to have an experience out of his body while he is living doesn't mean he will retain the same ability when dead. It may suggest that we are composed of body and soul, but it does not guarantee that the soul will survive.

Another puzzling feature of the near-death and deathbed accounts is the "encounter" with other beings. Many people report that they see others during their experience—often relatives and friends. Others speak of supernatural beings. How do we explain these?

Seeing Friends and Relatives

People on their deathbed or near death who return to report their OBE see departed friends and relatives who await their arrival in the beyond. Sometimes they merely see them at a distance beckoning and sometimes there is communication (usually nonverbal) between them. Let's look at some possible explanations.

In a few cases, there may be physiological and pharmacological explanations for the phenomenon. It is known that brain tumors as well as other phenomena generate visions of beings and sounds of voices.[42] But in most cases there was no medical indication that this might be the cause.

The study done by Osis and Haraldsson revealed that there were few physiological or pharmacological means to generate hallucinations. Of those who reported deathbed visions, only one in five was taking drugs such as morphine, fewer than one in ten had high fevers, and about one in ten had medical conditions (kidney failure, brain injury, stroke) that might cause hallucination. About two-thirds of the patients were entirely free of any medication that might be suspect.[43]

Some people argue that these lifelike appearances are a construct of the brain, some form of wish-fulfillment brought on by the stress of dying. Patients may also be reporting their interpretations rather than their actual experiences.

The following example provided by Dr. Charles Tart illustrates the problem of distorting interpretation:

> As an example, let us suppose that what really happens to a person is that he finds himself floating in the air above his body, in the middle of the night; while still surprised at this, he perceives a shadowy, dim figure at the end of the room, and then a blue circle of light floats past the figure from left to right. Then our experimenter loses consciousness and wakes up to find himself in his body. Many people will say, in perfect faith, something like, "My immortal soul was raised from the tomb of my body by the grace of God last night, and an angel appeared. As a symbol of God's favor, the angel showed me a symbol of wholeness."[44]

It is important, therefore that an interviewer do sufficient questioning to eliminate the possibility of the patient's reporting interpretation rather than actual experience. In many cases sufficient questioning has not been done, and we are receiving a heavy dose of interpretation and conclusion for very few uninterpreted facts.

In some cases there is evidence to support subjective interpretation and the wish-fulfillment hypothesis. For example, many of the visions have a strong cultural coloring. Osis and Haraldsson compared out-of-the-body accounts from India with those in the United States. What they found was that in many cases there was a strong cultural component in each group of visions.

In the United States, where the status of women is more equal to that of men than it is in India, 71 percent of the Americans saw females in their visions. In India, only 23 percent of all subjects saw females, and of the men, only 17 percent saw females.[45] Thus the lower status of women in India seems to correlate well with the reduced incidence of women in the visions.

It should be pointed out that not all the people seen in visions are dead. About 90 percent of the mothers, fathers, and siblings and 70 percent of the spouses and offspring were dead.[46] Whether this is significant depends on whether we can determine if those who saw living relatives were hallucinating or experiencing a real phenomenon. In general, patients with a medical history of hallucinations had visions that were more rambling, disjointed, and concerned with this-world purposes.[47] Thus we should eliminate them from the paranormal catagory, since they may have normal, medical explanations.

But even when we do consider all of the possible normal explanations (physiological, psychological, and pharmacological), we do not have enough to explain all the experiences. In fact, as we will see in the next chapter, there may even be paranormal explanations for those that seem to have a psychological explanation influenced by culture.

One reason they have to have some paranormal explanation is that there is no possible cause-effect relationship. It is very difficult to correlate the actions of these beings—sometimes called "take-away figures"—with any desire on the part of the person seeing the vision. As Dr. Osis puts it, "If the take-away figures were merely wish-fulfillment, we would find that they would come more often to patients who were expecting to die, and less often to those who thought they would recover. But there was, in fact, no such relationship."[48]

Another reason for a paranormal explanation is that those seeing others in their visions know information they could not obtain by normal means. Just as OBE reports revealed that people had access to knowledge that they could not have obtained in the normal way, so also these people report knowing things they could not have learned by normal means.

Examples of this are the reports by deathbed patients of seeing people they did not know were dead. The classic case of this can be found in Sir William Barrett's book *Death-bed Visions*, written in 1926. His wife, a physician specializing in obstetrical surgery, described the vision of Doris, a dying woman who had just given birth. Her sister Vida had died three weeks earlier, but this news had been kept from Doris because of her serious illness. While she was dying, she began speaking to a vision of her deceased father. Just before she died, the following conversation took place:

> She spoke to her father, saying, "I am coming," turning at the same time to look at me, saying, "Oh, he is so near." On looking at the same place again, she said with a rather puzzled expression, "He has Vida with him," turning again to me saying, "Vida is with him." Then she said, "You do want me, Dad; I am coming."[49]

Another example of this type was viewed by Natalie Kalmus (Hollywood technicolor expert) as her sister was dying. Miss Kalmus promised that no drugs would be administered to her sister, and as she sat with her sister on her deathbed, she described the following:

> I sat on her bed and took her hand. It was on fire, Then she seemed to rise up in bed almost to a sitting position. "Natalie!" she said. "There are so many of them. There's Fred . . . and Ruth. . . . What's she doing here? Oh, I know!"

An electric shock went through me. She had said "Ruth." Ruth was her cousin who had died suddenly the week before. But she had not been told of Ruth's sudden death. Chill after chill went up and down my spine. I felt on the verge of some powerful, almost frightening knowledge. She had murmured Ruth's name. Her voice was so surprisingly clear. "It's so confusing! So many of them!" Suddenly her arms stretched out happily as when she had welcomed me. "I'm going up," she said.[50]

A second type of example of unusual knowledge can be seen in the near-death encounter of Charles McKaig. After being resuscitated a number of times by Dr. Maurice Rawlings, he had a pleasant experience in which he saw his mother for the first time. She had died at the age of twenty-one when he was fifteen months old. Yet during his experience he knew it was his mother, even though he had not seen a picture of her. A few weeks later he was able to pick out a picture of her when he was at his mother's sister's house.[51]

In conclusion, there may be normal explanations for seeing some of the people, but in other cases there must be some paranormal explanation as well. The patient's knowledge of events and circumstances is too great to be accounted for on the basis of hallucinations and natural phenomena alone.

In the next chapter, we will look at some of these paranormal explanations, but let us first look at the phenomenon of the being of light some people report seeing.

The Light at the End of the Tunnel

Occasionally people report seeing spiritual beings in their visions. One of the most frequent reports in near-death accounts is a description of a being of light. What possible explanations are there for these reports of spiritual beings?

The presence of light is a feature reported in a variety of contexts. For example, practitioners of many of the Eastern religions note that during periods of meditation or yoga they may see a vision or a being of light. Whether what is described in these reports is the being of light seen in out-of-the-body experiences is doubtful.

In religious contexts in which drugs are used, such as the peyote rites of many American Indians, spiritual beings are often seen. Many of the same experiences that are achieved with peyote are reported by those who have had a near-death encounter, including meetings with other spiritual beings.[52]

But these experiences do not explain why people report seeing spiritual beings. The explanations are not physiological or pharmacological. They are paranormal in some cases and psychological in others.

Like the visions of friends and relatives, these spiritual visions have a strong cultural component to them. In citing the crosscultural studies done in the United States and India, Daniel Goleman noted:

> There was a strong cultural stamp to the visions. Most Americans saw loved ones, most Indians saw religious figures. Religion determined the identity of the figure; no Christian patient saw a Hindu deity, and no Hindu saw Jesus.[53]

In general, if an American saw a spiritual being he would think it was God, Jesus, or perhaps Mary. Indians saw either Lord Krishna or Yama, the lord of death.[54]

It is, unsatisfactory, however, to conclude that all these visions were culturally induced psychological phenomena. While initial studies seemed to indicate that only religious persons had visions of spiritual beings,[55] further studies showed that this was not always the case. What people see often cannot be correlated with expectation, belief, or wish-fulfillment. In many cases nonreligious people saw religious figures. As John White said, "The most extreme skeptic would not expect atheists to be happy about seeing, say, Jesus—yet that was just the case."[56]

The visions of spiritual beings are probably being interpreted according to the belief systems of the individuals. For example, a Jewish man and woman identified the being of light as an "angel."[57] Those with a Catholic background might say they saw Mary. Others might say that they saw spiritual beings like God, or Jesus, or departed religious figures like saints or prophets.[58]

While there is some correlation between the beliefs of the individual and the interpretations, there are exceptions. Atheists, though they might say they did not believe in religious beings, often perceived the being of light as a religious figure.[59] Some who identified themselves as Christians felt no compulsion to call the light "Christ."[60]

In general those who had these spiritual visions tended to interpret them in a spiritual way. The conclusions were often more dogmatic than the data would permit. When Dr. Kubler-Ross was asked about the identity of the being of light, she responded: "That light is God. . . . God is the light and love these people experience. They are entering His presence. That, for me, is beyond the shadow of a doubt."[61] Such confidence is typical. We often get a large dose of conclusion from a small amount of data.

As we have seen, there are some rather interesting things going on in these experiences. In some cases the only explanations that fit the data are that these are paranormal occurrences. But to base a belief in life after death on these paranormal experiences is unwise. Yet that is exactly what many have done.

Kubler-Ross stated one evening at a speaking engagement that all human beings make the transformation from death to a fuller life beyond the grave. According to her, "It's not a matter of belief or opinion. I know beyond a shadow of a doubt that there is life after death."[62]

Though she did not mean to make such a statement in

101

public, and we may be saddened that such statements by her have hurt her standing in the medical community, we must also realize how dangerous a statement it was. The statement came in response to a question asked by a woman who had lost a young child. While it is noble that she would want to compassionately assure this mother that there is life after death, she has claimed proof for life after death on controversial evidence.

Raymond Moody comes to the same basic conclusion. Though he is more cautious in his conclusions, he also sees the evidence as supporting life after death. He says, "I have come to accept as a matter of religious faith that there is life after death, and I believe that the phenomenon we have been examining is a manifestation of that life."[63]

Such statements have caused a dichotomy in our society. Scientists and doctors disagree with these claims on the basis of the data. Dr. Charles Garfield of the Cancer Research Institute of the University of California says, "I don't at all agree with Elisabeth [Kubler-Ross] when she says that the experiences she and I have both had working with the dying absolutely guarantee life after death."[64]

On the other hand, the lay public often accepts such conclusions almost without question. Since many already want to believe in life after death, they accept the conclusions. Basically they say, "Well, if Dr. Kubler- Ross says there is life after death, then it must be so."[65] Because of the trust the public has in the scientific community, people are willing to accept even the spiritual conclusions of Moody and Kubler-Ross.

A report from one of Robert Monroe's workshops illustrates this fact. A physician from Washington, D.C., when he was interviewed, asked, "Why do I pursue this?" His answer was, "Because I trust Kubler-Ross. She says it [an OBE] happens, so I believe it happens."[66] His trust as a doctor was based on her well-known experience with dying patients. He was willing to translate that trust in the area of science into the spiritual area as well.

Since there are so many claims being made for these experiences because of their paranormal nature, it is important to look at these paranormal claims in greater detail from a spiritual perspective. Let us see how these claims and experiences fit into a biblical understanding of life, death, and the world beyond.

SIX

PARANORMAL EXPERIENCES

What are we to make of paranormal experiences? Is there an answer that will encompass all of the data? Are we getting the whole picture when we hear these near-death and deathbed accounts? In this chapter we will explore paranormal experiences in an effort to provide a more accurate definition of death, give some explanation for paranormal experiences, and take a more detailed look at the world beyond death. But before we do so, let us look more closely at what is being claimed for these experiences.

Implications and Interpretations

In any area in which claims are being made, it is always wise to see how extensive the data is for the claim. Claims made from a limited or biased sample are not of much use either scientifically or statistically.

It is estimated that more than a thousand people a year have encounters with death and live to tell about it, being revived largely because of our advanced resuscitation techniques.[1] About one-fifth of those resuscitated report some afterlife experience.[2] Thus when we compare the number of people who have had experiences to the number that have been reported by investigators, we see a large discrepancy. The conclusions have been based on only a very small sample of the available data.

It is also difficult to achieve objectivity. For one thing, the previous medical or psychological history of the patient and his identity have been kept confidential. It is impossible to verify the investigator's work. In addition, adequate efforts have not been made to eliminate, as much as possible, the subject's subjectivity. For example, the initial experience was recorded in the person's memory. Only at some later date (which in some cases is years) is the event retrieved to be reported. Over a period of time any experience is subject to different perceptual grids that will color the final telling of the event. Again, in the investigator's interpreting, cataloging, and correlating the data, a lot of room for error is possible. The flow of the information might look something like this:

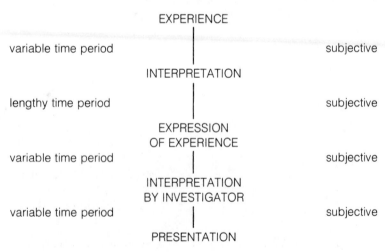

Given the problems this type of research is fraught with, we should not yet expect very much in the way of definitive conclusions. But quite incredible claims are already being made from these paranormal experiences.

In most cases people are using these experiences to validate their own world view. They see them as a vindication of their personal perspectives. As one article put it,

> Christians testify to seeing Christ while Hindus say they come face to face with Krishna. Cultists tend to have their world view validated, and some nominal Christians adopt heterodox opinions. A Scottish Presbyterian, for example, testified: "I know beyond a doubt that the Christ I saw will accept everyone, good or bad."[3]

People are usually convinced "beyond a doubt" by these experiences that their views are correct.

In other cases these experiences have changed people's perspectives. Views they formerly held dear now have given way to new ideas more in line with their experience. An article about George Ritchie (to whom Raymond Moody dedicated his book) illustrates this change:

> He says his previous concept of death and life afterward will never be the same. He was raised in a "strict orthodox Southern Baptist" home when "the idea pretty much was that if you died you went to heaven or you went to hell." Today he belongs to the Methodist church but describes himself as an "ecumenist."[4]

Such shifts in beliefs are not uncommon.

In fact, these experiences virtually open the door to almost any belief system. Once these experiences are considered definitive by the general public, who knows where they will lead? As Charles Garfield noted, "People are talking about this subject to a public that is thirsting for it. It's not really fair. Soon you'll get six thousand grandmothers in Des Moines starting a cult."[5]

Part of the problem stems from a misunderstanding of the field of epistemology (the study of how we know). Basically there are three major ways in which we can learn things about the world. We can learn by *experience* and the use of our senses. We can learn by *experiment* and scientific investigation. And we can learn by *revelation*—that is, by being told.

There is, as well, a hierarchy of these three modes of learning. What we learn by experience should always be verified by further experiment. We may think we see water in the desert. But before we conclude it is there, we should do further experiments to make sure that it is not a mirage. So must we interpret our experiences in the light of revelation.

When we find that our experiences contradict biblical revelation, we should put the burden of proof on our experience, not on the Bible. If the Bible is God's revealed truth, as it claims to be, we should not expect it to be wrong.

Unfortunately, what is happening is that people are willing to accept subjective experiences and to reject objective biblical revelation. People are often willing to trust their eternal destinies to claims based on their paranormal experiences.

Since we are dealing with paranormal claims, the best way we can examine them is to compare them to biblical statements about the nature of paranormal places and events. Whenever there is a contradiction, our best approach is to consider the experience suspect and examine it more closely.

But first, let us look more closely at the definition of death.

The Biblical Definition of Death

The Bible makes definitive statements about death. Death is more than just a biological event. The Bible describes both the physical and the spiritual aspects of death. It is normal and paranormal, and it involves both the body and the soul. Thus a proper definition of death requires more than just biological data. It requires a spiritual perspective that can be found by looking at the biblical definition of death.

Whenever anyone begins a discussion of a biblical definition of death, one of the first verses mentioned is 2 Corinthians

5:8. Paul says that he would prefer to be "away from the body and to be at home with the Lord." Though many have interpreted this verse as saying that death is instantaneous and total, the context does not necessarily warrant such an interpretation. It is simply Paul's statement that he is willing to die that he might be present with the Lord. Death could be either an instantaneous event or a lengthy process.

The early Jewish concept was that it was a process rather than an event. In fact Jews believed that death was not complete for a number of days. According to Alfred Edersheim,

> It was the common Jewish idea that corruption commenced on the fourth day, that the drop of gall, which had fallen from the sword of the Angel and caused death, was then working its effect, and that, as the face changed, the soul took its final leave from the resting-place of the body.[6]

Thus it was a common Jewish notion that death was complete when the soul left the body on the fourth day. It is no wonder that when Jesus raised Lazarus after he lay dead in the tomb for four days the Jews were so shocked (John 11:17). They saw it as more than a mere resuscitation.

This Jewish view is not the view one gets from a complete survey of what the Bible says about death, however. A direct correlation is made between the leaving of man's spirit and his physical death. When the spirit leaves the body, a person dies physically.

This is best illustrated by Psalm 146:4: "When their spirit departs, they return to the ground." The departing of a person's spirit indicates death. Death, according to Ecclesiastes 12:7, is a process that has two stages. First, the body "returns to the ground it came from" (see Gen. 3:19). Second, the spirit of man "returns to God who gave it."

Once the spirit separates from the body, death is irreversible. The Bible clearly states that, apart from the miraculous intervention of God, death cannot then be reversed. When we die, we are "like water spilled on the ground, which cannot be recovered" (2 Sam. 14:14). Hebrews 9:27 says that "man is destined to die once, and after that to face judgment."

But if death is followed by judgment, why didn't any of those who had near-death experiences say anything about it? The answer lies in the biblical definition of death. These people did not encounter any judgment because they did not die. They had a near-death encounter, but their spirit did not permanently separate from their bodies.

At this point there might be some confusion. One might ask, Doesn't the fact that these people had out-of-body experiences imply that their spirit separated from their bodies? The surprising answer is no.

Those who have been involved in research on out-of-body experiences have noted a very interesting phenomenon. Even when a person is having an OBE, he is still in contact with his body. He is attached to his body by means of a "cord." On one of his out-of-body excusions, Robert Monroe describes looking for the cord that connected his physical body with his Second Body:

> I turned to look for the "cord" but it was not visible to me; either it was too dark or not there. Then I reached around my head to see if I could feel it coming out the front, top, or back of my head. As I reached the back of my head, my hands brushed against something and I felt behind me with both hands. Whatever it was extended out from a spot in my back directly between my shoulder blades. . . . I reached outward, and it formed into a "cord," if you can call a two-inch-thick cable a "cord."[7]

Such a phenomenon is not limited to out-of-body experiences. It has also been reported by those at a deathbed.

> The claims of those who say that they have had out-of-the-body experiences are further corroborated to some extent by some death-bed phenomena. There are on record instances where the

by-standers say that, shortly before death, they have seen a second body rising in a misty form from the recumbent body of the patient. They say, moreover, that the two bodies are joined together by a silver cord.[8]

There have been many reports of this cord that attaches the physical to the nonphysical. It has been described as a "slight cord," a "cloudy-looking cord," a "shining white cord," or a "strand."[9] The Tibetans called it "an almost impalpable cord." Dr. Kubler-Ross has called it a type of "umbilical cord." But the most common description of the cord is that it is a "silver" or "silvery" cord.[10]

Though there is some slight disagreement concerning its description, there is no doubt that when the cord is broken, death results. This testimony by Dr. R. B. Hout at his aunt's deathbed is typical:

> As I watched the suspended spirit body, my attention was called, again intuitively, to a silverlike substance that was streaming from the head of the physical body to the head of the spirit "double." Then I saw the connection-cord between the two bodies. As I watched, the thought, "The silver cord!" kept running through my mind. I knew, for the first time, the meaning of it. This "silver cord" was the connecting-link between the physical and the spirit bodies, even as the umbilical cord unites the child to its mother. . . . The last connecting strand of the silver cord snapped and the spirit body was free.[11]

Thus when the silver cord is broken, the spirit leaves the body permanently, and the physical body dies.

It is an interesting conclusion. It is interesting, first, because it helps to answer the question why the Bible describes death as irreversible. Once the cord is broken or severed, the spirit leaves the body, and death occurs. It is also interesting because it is a conclusion that may not be new. In fact, it appears that it may have been written down first thousands of years ago.

In Ecclesiastes 12:6–7, we find these verses on the subject of death and its definition:

> Remember him [your Creator]—before the *silver cord is severed,* or the golden bowl is broken; before the pitcher is shattered at the spring, or the wheel broken at the well, and the dust *returns to the ground* it came from, and the *spirit returns to God* who gave it (italics added).

The poetical language makes these verses difficult to interpret exactly; however, it has been suggested in the past that the silver cord in this passage refers to the spinal cord,[12] or that it is a symbol for the loss of life support.[13] Perhaps, in the light of the above reports it might be suggested that the silver cord described in Ecclesiastes is the silver cord that is broken or severed at the point of irreversible death. Whatever it is meant to symbolize, its breaking seems to be a picture of death.

We conclude that a biblical description of death does not contradict some of the data produced by these near-death and death-bed accounts. Death occurs when the spirit is separated from the body.

Let us now look more closely at these out-of-body experiences. Not only do they tell us something about the nature of the world, but they also tell us a great deal about the nature of the human being. Let us take another look at this ghost in the machine called man.

The Ghost in the Machine

One of the great philosophical debates of the ages concerns the question, What is man? Philosophers have debated whether man is merely a material creature or whether he is more. Those philosophers who were materialists and denied that man has a spiritual nature saw man as only a machine. In this regard, philosopher Gilbert Ryle said of man: "There is no ghost in the machine."[14]

Materialists have understood man as composed entirely of the material elements of the earth. The German philosopher Feuerbach said that "man is what he eats."[15] In other words, we are composed of nothing but chemicals. There is no spirit; there is no soul. Man is a body and nothing more.

Many people cannot accept the notion that man is merely material. They believe he is something more. When we look at a dead body, we get an uncanny feeling. It is not just that it looks peaceful. It is more that it looks vacant. No one is "at home." The face may be the same, but the person is gone.

From this intuitive notion, as well as from other data, comes evidence that man is both material and immaterial. He is both a body and a soul, a brain and a mind. To answer Gilbert Ryle, there *is* a ghost in the human machine.

But this is not exactly right. Man is not merely a container for a spirit. Actually he is a spirit. He is not made up of two independent, autonomous parts. He is a whole and a unity of these parts. Genesis 2:7 teaches that man is a living soul. He does not contain a soul but rather is a soul. He is literally ensouled flesh.

Such a view of man suggests why earlier experiments to weigh the soul have met with complete failure. Attempts to weigh the body before and after death to·see if there was a change in weight were ill-conceived. It would make about as much sense to measure a sense of humor, a feeling of love, or a joyful experience.

We should also note that people are not really ghosts in machines, for not only are they not *in* machines, they are also not *machines*. They are free moral agents, not preprogrammed, determined biological machines.[16] Rather, they have been created in the image of God (Gen. 1:27) and have been made just "a little lower than the heavenly beings" (Ps. 8:5). There are physical, psychological, and social distinctions between man and the rest of the living world.

113

If we look at the Bible to see what it says about mankind, we find some fascinating information. We are described as being composed of body, soul, and spirit. We have a material part (the body) and an immaterial part (the soul and spirit). Some commentators have held that the Bible teaches that soul and spirit are basically synonymous, while others feel they are distinct and different.

While it must be admitted that the dichotomous view, which argues that we have a material and an immaterial nature, has some merit, some verses seem to indicate that man is composed of three parts. First Thessalonians 5:23 lists body, soul, and spirit as separate entities. The Bible also uses different words for soul and spirit. If both words refer to the same thing, it is difficult to see why different words are used, often in different contexts. In addition, Hebrews 4:12 talks about "dividing soul and spirit," though some would see "soul" and "spirit" as synonyms in this verse.

It should be pointed out in passing that although "spirit" and "soul" could also be translated "breath," this does not imply that the context in every instance would warrant it. If in every verse these words could also be translated "breath," it could be said that the Bible may not be teaching that man is more than matter. This is not the case, however. One need only try to substitute the word *breath* for the word *spirit* in verses like Acts 23:8–9; 1 Corinthians 5:5; and Galatians 6:18 or for *soul* in verses like Psalm 19:7; 1 Thessalonians 5:23; and 2 Peter 2:8 to see how impossible such a substitution is.

Let us now see how the biblical view of the nature of man fits with our discussion about death. First, it is the giving of this "breath" or "spirit" that makes man conscious (Gen. 2:7). As long as his spirit is intact, he is a conscious being. Second, when this spirit leaves the body, death results (Ps. 146:6; Eccl. 12:7; Luke 23:46; James 2:26).

We now need to consider the distinction between resuscitation and resurrection. As a working definition, we can define a resurrection as a miraculous event that brings a person who is truly dead (in the biblical sense) back to life. A resuscitation is an event (miraculous or otherwise) that returns a person from a near-death encounter.

Using these definitions, we can probably isolate several bona fide resurrections in the Bible. Elijah brought the widow's son (1 Kings 17:17–24) and the Shunammite's son (2 Kings 4:32) back to life. Also in the Old Testament is the account of the resurrection of the prophet who was buried in the grave of Elisha (2 Kings 13:20). In the New Testament, Jesus raised Jairus's daughter (Mark 5:21–24), the son of the widow of Nain (Luke 7:11–15), and Lazarus (John 11:1–44).

One incident that could best be described as a resuscitation is the account of Eutychus in Acts 20:9–12. After he had fallen from a window, he was pronounced dead (v. 9), but Paul declared that his *soul* was still in him (v. 10). Relating this fact to our previous discussion, we may conclude that consciousness was lost because the spirit was disengaged. Yet we find that his *soul* was still in him because his spirit had not broken away from his body. The momentary separation of the spirit from the body did not break the bond that unites the body with the soul.

This notion is further illuminated by Hebrews 4:12 in which the relationship of the soul and the spirit are compared to joints and marrow. Just as joints and marrow produce physical activity, so the soul and spirit produce the activity of our heart (thoughts and attitudes). It is the interaction of the spirit with the soul that produces consciousness and "heart." Thus it is the union of the spirit with the body and soul that gives us our intellect, emotion, and will (in essence, our personality).

When the spirit is disengaged, it is possible for a person to exist outside his body if he is still attached to his soul. Out-of-body experiences are probably one example of this possibility. When the spirit separates completely from the body, death results, and man's soul is withdrawn to another place where it can resume consciousness. According to 2 Corinthians 5:8, to be absent from the body is, for the believer, to be present with the Lord.

OBEs give us an interesting insight into human nature. Because we are both a physical and spiritual being, we may under certain circumstances have experiences out of our bodies. Thus we should not be surprised that someone who has been resuscitated can recount everything that happened while he was "unconscious." Understanding human nature helps to explain many of these paranormal cases.

It does not explain all such cases, however. Even when we look at the various explanations and examine the definition of death and human nature, we cannot account for every detail reported. In some of the cases direct spiritual intervention is the only explanation.

Spiritual Contact

In some cases those who are experiencing near-death and deathbed encounters make contact with the spiritual world. Their experiences do not have normal, natural explanations. They are paranormal and they are a result of direct contact with the eternal world. Let us look at these in more detail from a biblical perspective.

A number of researchers in the field have seen these contacts as indicating something of the nature of the afterlife and the unity of the world religions. For example, psychiatrist Stanislav Grof of the Maryland Psychiatric Research Center has been doing work with altered states of consciousness. He has studied these states through the use of drugs and OBEs. When he gives LSD to dying patients, he finds some interesting results:

They progress through several stages. At the last they have mystical experiences that Grof recognizes as similar to those "described for millennia in various temple mysteries, initiation rites and occult religions." Such experiences, Grof concludes, are intrinsic to human nature and "suggest the possibility of bridging the gap between contemporary science and ancient wisdom."[17]

Such a conclusion is very interesting. The experiences seem to parallel ancient wisdom and are gained through paranormal contact. The mystical experiences people report have been gained through means different from those that have traditionally been the means of contacting the spiritual world, but they seem to agree closely with our earlier conclusion. As parapsychologist John White put it:

> Previously in parapsychology, the emphasis was on what mediums had to say. Here we had a chance to look at the same problem through the eyes of the dying in two widely divergent cultures. This gives us a better idea of what might be there, and it also tends to confirm much of the picture gained through mediumship.[18]

But the practice of necromancy (consulting the spirits of the dead through mediums) is just one piece of evidence cited by parapsychologists to prove that there is life after death. In their book *At the Hour of Death*, Osis and Haraldsson list five major categories that provide evidence of the afterlife. These categories are:

1. Mediumship
2. Apparitions, especially those seen by several observers
3. Reincarnation memories
4. Out-of-body experiences
5. Deathbed observations[19]

As we have already pointed out, these areas are open to some question.* Most of these experiences can be explained apart from the conclusion that there is life after death. Most of

---

*Although memories of previous incarnations have not been dealt with so far, appendix 1 analyzes these reincarnation experiences (see pp. 169ff.).

them can be explained by natural means. Also, because they are based on the subjective experiences of others, the information is not totally reliable. Embellishment and suppression of information are very real possibilities.

Yet in spite of these inherent difficulties, some experimenters cite these experiences as evidence for the afterlife. The primary reason they do so is that these experiences are so similar to each other from one culture and religion to another. As Moody puts it, "It is amazing to hear a person who has never read a thing about mysticism relate his near-death experience to you; the similarities transcend cultures and time."[20]

One book in particular is cited quite regularly. It is the *Tibetan Book of the Dead.* The parallels between it and contemporary near-death reports are astounding. Though written long ago, it describes after-death experiences that are remarkably similar to those reported in hospitals today. Events during and after death are broken into periods called "bardos." These bardo experiences begin when a person is dying and continue for the next forty-nine days. The sounds one hears and the light one sees are mentioned. Heavens and hells, demons and Buddhas are supposed to represent various stages of the mind. The bardos even recreate the major mental states, habits, and memories of the person who is dying.

In the midst of these similarities we must ask an important question. Do these similarities exist because these people are all seeing a true picture of the afterlife or because they are receiving a common counterfeit picture? Either is possible. What is assumed on the part of these researchers is that because so many people see the same thing, it must represent a genuine picture of reality. The other perspective, however, is just as reasonable. A number of men might be lost in a desert and all agree that they see water on the horizon. Just because they all think they see it does not discount the very real possibility that they are simply seeing a mirage. A simple consensus does not necessarily tell you very much about the truth.

A similar distortion may be taking place here. In fact as we try to place these experiences in a biblical framework, we find that a spiritual counterfeit is a very real possibility. Let's see why.

First, the report each person gives of his experience differs from that of others. Though we might recognize similarities, it is the differences that cause problems. As we have already pointed out, each person sees a being in keeping with his cultural and religious background. If he expects to see an angel, he will see an angel. If he expects to see Lord Krishna, he will see Lord Krishna. But though cultural interpretation may be a factor, there are cases where it would not be reasonable to make such an assumption.

The differences cause the problems. If people had perceived the same reality, their reports would generally agree with each other. But though there is a broad agreement, rarely is there much agreement on specifics. One would expect there to be more agreement on the actual phenomena occurring at death, just as one would expect some degree of agreement between two witnesses of the same automobile accident. But there is not.

Second, the reports contradict the Bible. They do not agree with biblical statements about the nature of life after death and the attributes of God. Whereas the Bible describes both heaven and hell, bliss and judgment, people uniformly report a pleasant experience. Whereas the Bible describes God as a holy and righteous being, those with near-death encounters often speak of a humorous and flippant being of light.

Third, one gets a definite feeling that much of the experience is staged for the benefit of the near-death adventurer. Granted that this is an intuitive judgment, one cannot help but have the feeling after listening to many of the cases. They are too perfect, too easy, too much what people want to hear. It is like listening to a political candidate make promises to end economic distress and unemployment. It is certainly what we want to hear, but wishing it were true won't make it true. We might wish that life on the other side of the grave were a pleasant experience for all, but it is only a wish and not an established fact.

One is also struck by the fact that those who experience these paranormal phenomena are instructed to return. Often the being of light or some inner force compels them to bring back "news from the other side." A nurse who had such an experience now shares this pleasant news with the dying patients she is counseling. She says, "When you've had the experience, there is a compulsion to share it. It's almost as though you felt that you were meant to return to tell about it."[21]

As we look at this information "from the other side," we note that it does indeed parallel what we have learned from mediums as they consult other spirits. Therefore it would be good to view it in the context of mediumship and other activities of the occult. If there is a connection, there is great cause for alarm.

The Bible is particularly harsh in its condemnation of those who practice necromancy. Though we might feel that it is just one more thing that "tolerant" and civilized people should allow and not condemn, the Bible clearly forbids it. In Deuteronomy 18:9-13 it is listed as one of the most detestable of practices, along with such other practices as human sacrifice.

Accepting this judgment for the moment, how does it fit with these reports? First, most of those involved in death research (thanatology) are also involved in studies of parapsychology and the occult. In fact, many are involved in some form of occult practice (often necromancy). For example, Martin Ebon, who wrote *The Evidence for Life after Death*, also wrote books on parapsychology like *They Knew the Unknown* and *Prophecy in Our Time* and edited books like *Beyond Space and Time: An ESP Casebook* and *The Psychic Reader*. Susy Smith wrote not only *Out-of-Body Travel* but also books on automatic writing, ESP, hypnosis, and reincarnation. Similar statements can be made for other researchers such as Robert Crookall, Karlis Osis, and Allen Spraggett.

What is even more interesting is that some members of the medical profession who have written about near-death experiences, notably Kubler-Ross and Moody, are also in contact with spirits. Though one may be greatly impressed with the medical credentials and achievements of Kubler-Ross, one cannot help but be concerned that she has become more and more involved in occult activities.

One of the first public announcements of such activities came at a lecture she gave to an audience composed primarily of physicians and health-care professionals. Though they came to hear about her medical insights, the audience of seventy-five instead heard about her life and especially her spiritual and mystical experiences. She said:

> Last night I was visited by Salem, my spirit guide, and two of his companions, Anka and Willie. They were with us until three o'clock in the morning. We talked, laughed and sang together. They spoke and touched me with the most incredible love and tenderness imaginable. This was the highlight of my life.[22]

Since that time, these spiritual beings have appeared to Kubler-Ross and serve as her personal guides. Greater detail about her companionship with these spirits appeared in an article in *Human Behavior*.[23] She tells of her relationship with them and even played tapes of Willie for the interviewer.

Dr. Moody, though he does not publicize his experiences as Kubler-Ross does, also has been involved with spirits. He has had great interest in various esoteric philosophies (Eastern, occultic, and psychic). But his interest is more than merely academic. It has been reported that he too had a spirit that he has regularly conversed with about a variety of topics, including the arrangement of flowers on the University of Virginia campus.[24]

We see, therefore, that there is a connection between some researchers of these phenomena and the occult. But what is of even greater importance is the evidence that many of the extremely unusual experiences those who have been resuscitated report may, in fact, be counterfeit spiritual encounters.

Although the Bible describes the spiritual realm, it also notes that it can be and has been counterfeited. Just as God exists, so does Satan. Jesus said that "there is no truth in him. When he lies, he speaks his native language, for he is a liar and the father of lies" (John 8:44). Satan is the master of deception, the father of lies, and the origin of all spiritual counterfeits.

In this context, it is not difficult to see that Satan may be involved. First, some encounter a being of light. Each perceives the being in a different way, but all describe him as a warm light. Second, they see others (usually friends and relatives) who also bring them messages of hope or righteousness.

It is interesting that in turning to 2 Corinthians 11:14–15 we read that "Satan himself masquerades as an angel of light" while "his servants masquerade as servants of righteousness." The being of light and the other people seen in these paranormal experiences could indeed be Satan and his fellow demons who are working to perpetrate a spiritual hoax on those who are near death and on the living who hear these reports.

In his book *Life After Life*, Raymond Moody considers such a possibility but immediately dismisses it because "Satan would presumably tell his servants to follow a course of hate and destruction."[25] Since his patients returned to follow a course of love and a quest for knowledge, he assumes that such a possibility is remote.

However, if one studies the character of Satan, it can be seen that such a conclusion does not necessarily follow. He is not the pointed-tailed, pitchfork-carrying creature that many envision. Rather he is described as a very beautiful angel who rebelled against God in attempting to make himself higher than God (Isa. 14:4–14). His strategy is to use intelligent, cunning maneuvers to gain his control. To assume that a satanic counterfeit would make people return to follow a course of hate and destruction is to grossly underestimate the being called our adversary (1 Peter 5:8).

There are ways we can discern whether these experiences are spiritually counterfeited. The especially helpful paper "Criteria for the Discerning of Spirits" establishes criteria along with guidelines for applying them. It forms part of a collection of papers presented at a symposium on demon possession under the auspices of the Christian Medical Association.[26] The paranormal experiences we have been describing fit the criteria given for determining spiritual counterfeits.

Apart from this theological argument, there is further evidence to support the notion that these experiences are spiritual counterfeits. According to various literatures, demons have the ability to transform themselves into other forms in order to deceive. The cultural and personal overtones of many of these experiences may result from this deception rather than from the cultural grid and subsequent interpretation of the observer.

One example of this demonic transformation comes from Robert Monroe. On one of his out-of-body excursions he encountered some rather interesting creatures as he explains in the following report:

> I started out carefully—and felt something on my back! I remembered the little fellow from before, and certainly didn't want to try to go somewhere with him hanging on my back. . . . Then, as I was trying to hold off the first, a second climbed on my back! Holding

the first off with one hand, I reached back and yanked the second off me, and floated over into the center of the office, holding one in each hand, screaming for help. I got a good look at each, and as I looked, each turned into a good facsimilie of one of my two daughters (the psychiatrist will have a good time with this one)! I seemed to know immediately that this was a deliberate camouflage on their parts to create emotional confusion in me and call on my love for my daughters to prevent me from doing anything to them. The moment I realized the trick, the two no longer appeared to be my daughters. . . . Then I saw someone else coming up out of the corner of my eye. I first thought it was another one, but this was very definitely a man. He simply stopped a short distance away and watched what was taking place with a very serious expression on his face. I got a very good look at him. First, his eyes were very familiar to me. They reminded me somewhat of a paternal cousin's, light in color, a little sunken. He has his hair cut evenly around his head, including bangs across the forehead, and short across the pate, almost bald. He wore a dark robe down to his ankles. I could not see his feet.[27]

Here in the midst of an out-of-body experience Monroe saw people who appeared to be his relatives. He noted the ability of the two "little fellows" to transform themselves at will. He also noted the man's resemblance to that of his paternal cousin. Although Monroe would not have been considered clinically dead, he had visions that parallel those reported by people on their deathbed or near death.

Another example of demonic transformation comes, in a sense, "from the horse's mouth." In the book *Seth Speaks* there is a story of one such demonic transformation. What is interesting is that the book is actually supposedly written by a spirit named Seth. While Jane Roberts was in a trance, Seth took over her body, and Jane's husband wrote down the material in the book as Seth spoke it.

The book deals with many topics, including a commentary on the "death" experience. In that chapter, Seth describes some of his responsibilities when death comes. The following description concerns an Arab who was being put to death:

> The Arab was a very interesting character, by the way, and to illustrate some of the difficulties involved, I will tell you about him. He hated the Jews, but somehow was obsessed with the idea that Moses was more powerful than Allah, and for years this was the secret sin upon his conscience. . . . He cried to Allah, and then in greater desperation to Moses, and as his consciousness left his body, Moses was there.
>
> He believed in Moses more than he did Allah, and I did not know until the last moment which form I was to assume. He was a very likable chap, and under the circumstances I did not mind when he seemed to expect a battle for his soul. Moses and Allah were to fight for him. . . .
>
> A friend and I, with some others, staged the ceremony, and from opposite clouds in the sky Allah and I shouted out our claims upon his soul—while he, poor man, cowered on the ground between us. Now while I tell this story humorously, you must understand that the man's belief brought it about, and so to set him free, we worked it through.[28]

Two most enlightening things emerge from this report. First, Seth was able to transform himself into either Moses or Allah. This ability, which is apparently instantaneous, fits with 2 Corinthians 11:15. That verse notes that Satan's servants can transform themselves into servants of righteousness. Second, we note that it was the Arab's belief system that determined the transformation that would take place.

It therefore appears that these experiences in some cases are being counterfeited by spiritual beings. But an obvious question that arises is, Why are these experiences being counterfeited? The best answer to that question is that the true view of death and the afterlife must be hidden from human beings if Satan is to succeed in his task.

According to the Bible, when we turned against God, our rebellion led to the Fall (Gen. 3). Thus all suffering, decay, and even death are a result of that Fall. Since death is the major result of the Fall, it might be the final means that God uses to cause us to see our need of Him. If that conviction is short-circuited, we will be effectively cut off from seeing our need for God. That is one of Satan's goals.

In some cases people bring back messages from the being of light that contradict the Bible. This too is a tactic of Satan. It seems that Paul foresaw such a possibility when he said that even if "an angel from heaven should preach a gospel other than the one we preached to you, let him be eternally condemned!" (Gal. 1:8).

In conclusion, it is very likely that paranormal experiences are counterfeited by spiritual beings. This means that not all paranormal experiences are counterfeits. If there are counterfeits, the implication is that there are also true experiences. In order to tell the genuine from the counterfeit, we need to look at the biblical view of death and the life hereafter.

SEVEN

AFTERLIFE
EXPERIENCES

Once we turn from an analysis of paranormal experiences to those involving the afterlife, we immediately begin a journey into an area devoid of serious investigation but full of speculation. In order to keep our bearings, we need to have some standard with which to compare these experiences. Since there are afterlife experiences in the Bible, let us look at these in order to see what similarities and contrasts there may be.

The Biblical View of the Afterlife

Jesus in Luke's Gospel gives what may be the most complete picture of the afterlife. In Luke 16:19–31 He speaks of two men who encounter different fates on the other side of the grave. Although many believe this is simply a parable to illustrate one or two points of Jesus' teaching, it is more likely that this is a story by which Jesus teaches us many things about after-death experiences.

We are first introduced to a rich man who had "dressed in purple and fine linen and lived in luxury every day." The second character in the story is a poor man names Lazarus. He survived as a beggar by lying at the gate of the rich man in order to be fed the crumbs falling from the rich man's table. He may have been afflicted with some debilitating disease that prevented him from working and required that he be carried to the gate. The sores on his body not only racked his body with pain, but they marked him as a leper and made him a social outcast. The only attendance to his wounds came from the dogs that licked his sores.

Both men died. The story now shifts from the material realm to the spiritual realm and we begin to see what takes place once death occurs. When Lazarus died, "the angels carried him to Abraham's side" (v. 22).* When the rich man died, he found himself in Hades. Hades is divided into two sections: a place for the righteous dead (called paradise) and a place for the unrighteous dead. A great chasm separates the two, making it impossible to go from one to the other.

At the moment of death both men were instantaneously transported to their final destinations. There is no suggestion of a passage of time during which the soul might be asleep or in some state of limbo. When death occurred, Lazarus was carried by the angels to Abraham's side. The text does not tell us how the rich man got to Hades, but it is certainly not contrary to the text to assume that an angel or some other spirit took him there.

Though both men were physically dead, they were immediately conscious and in possession of a second body. The rich man "looked up"; he also mentioned parts of the body (e.g., the finger and the tongue). Thus descriptions of a physical nature are used.

Emotions are also mentioned. Lazarus was comforted at Abraham's side, whereas the rich man was in agony. He was in possession of his mental faculties as well. He saw, he recog-

*For the Jew, to be at Abraham's side was to be in paradise. Notice the correlation with John 1:18, which says that Jesus was at the Father's side before He came to earth.

nized, he felt, he pleaded, he was thirsty, he heard, he hoped, and he reasoned. All his major senses and intellectual capacities seemed to be intact. He even had a memory and was able to recall his past actions and the fact that he had five living brothers.

This story teaches that human beings have two different eternal destinations. Our faith and our activities on earth affect our eternal destiny. Once death takes place, there is nothing that can be done to change that destiny. We do not see the rich man pleading to be saved. He was resigned to his fate because he realized it was too late to cross the chasm that separated him from Lazarus and Abraham.

Another feature of the story is that it presents God as a God who judges. Contrary to the accounts of those who meet a benign being of light, the Bible talks about judgment. In the context of the story, Abraham declared God's judgment to the rich man and provided comfort to Lazarus (v. 25). A final judgment will take place in which the believer will stand before Christ's judgment seat (2 Cor. 5:10) and the unbeliever will stand before the great white throne (Rev. 20:11–15).

The rich man begged Abraham to send Lazarus back to his house to warn his five brothers. But Abraham made no attempt to communicate with them. There is no communication between the living and the dead. The Bible is a sufficient communication of God's will to man (v. 31).

Verse 31 contains an interesting statement. Basically it declares that if someone rejects revelation, experience (whether his own or that of another) will not cause him to believe. If the brothers will not "listen to Moses and the Prophets, they will not be convinced even if someone rises from the dead." This is certainly the testimony of both the Old and the New Testaments. In the Old Testament, King Saul did not repent at the sight of Samuel at Endor. In the New Testament, the Pharisees did not repent when they saw

Lazarus come out of the tomb. In fact when Jesus raised His friend Lazarus from the dead, they were driven to the height of unbelief and "plotted to take his life" (John 11:53).

We can reach five important conclusions from this story. First, there is conscious existence immediately after death. Second, there are both pleasant and unpleasant experiences after death. Third, it is not possible for the living to communicate with the dead (at least not to warn them to repent). Fourth, there is no chance to change one's eternal destiny once death occurs. Fifth, God's revelation is sufficient, and no experience will lead the confirmed skeptic to faith apart from it.

Let us examine this last conclusion in greater detail. Is revelation sufficient? How do I know it's true? Can I really trust what it says about life after death? Is there sufficient evidence for me to place my faith in it? We will now examine questions such as these.

How Can I Be Sure?

The Bible claims to be the Word of God. It does not claim to be a speculative scheme about the afterlife but rather information that was directly communicated to man by God (2 Tim. 3:16; 2 Peter 1:20–21). Now, such a claim is not self-authenticating; we can, and we should, test that claim.

Thus Christianity is unique in that it is based on a document that claims to be the Word of God. It is unique also in that it is based on the life and teaching of a founder who claimed to be God. No other founder of a major religion ever claimed to be God in the way Jesus did.

For example, Jesus claimed equality with God by making statements like these: "Anyone who has seen me has seen the Father" (John 14:9); "When a man believes in me, he does not believe in me only, but in the one who sent me" (John 12:44); and "Whoever welcomes me does not welcome me but the one who sent me" (Mark 9:37).

130

He also made many direct claims that indicated His belief in His divinity. He claimed to be the "I am" of the Old Testament (Exod. 3:14), the phrase on which the sacred name of God was based. As a result, the Jews sought to kill Him for blasphemy (John 8:24, 28, 58; 18:56). When He was confronted with the charge of blasphemy by the Jewish Sanhedrin, Jesus not only said He was God but said, quoting Psalm 110:1, that they would see Him sitting at God's right hand (Matt. 26:60–64; Mark 14:61–64; Luke 22:67–71). He also taught that He was the exclusive path to salvation: "I am the way and the truth and the life. No one comes to the Father except through me" (John 14:6).

Indirectly Jesus claimed to be God by doing things only God can do. For example, He forgave sins (Matt. 9:2–7; Mark 2:5–7; Luke 7:47–48). He taught that prayer should be in His name (John 16:23), He accepted worship as God (Matt. 14:33; Luke 5:8; John 20:28). He also claimed authority over the laws and institutions God had established (e.g., the temple in Matt. 12:6 and John 2:18, the sabbath in Matt. 12:8, and the Law in Matt. 5:31–34, 38–39).

We can be sure the events of the first century and particularly the sayings of Jesus were accurately reported in the Bible. First, the authors of the New Testament were eyewitnesses or else wrote down eyewitness accounts (Acts 1:1–3; 2 Peter 1:16). Thus, we do not have records from secondhand sources but from those who knew Jesus and the facts surrounding His ministry.

Furthermore, the New Testament writers appealed to the knowledge of their hearers concerning what had happened (Acts 2:22; 26:24–28). Any departure from the facts could easily have been corrected, especially when we realize that many of the hearers of the message of the early church were hostile to Christianity.

The Pharisees saw the first Christians as significant threats and did all within their power to crush the movement. The Saduccees, another sect of Jews, denied the existence of life after death and fought against the Christians for what they considered their heretical teachings.

Among the Greeks there were some who believed in the immortality of the soul but laughed at the notion of the resurrection of the body (Acts 17:32). Others, such as the Stoics, did not believe in life after death and also were not convinced by the presentations of the early Christians. And once the Romans saw that Christians were not just a Jewish sect, they persecuted them more than any of the other groups as a threat to their internal unity.

In the face of such hostility inaccuracies or distortions of fact would have been impossible. It is the striking testimony of the early church that there was never any reported disagreement about the facts. Any controversy centered on the interpretation of the facts, never on their accuracy.

Third, we can check the accuracy of the record by consulting extrabiblical documents and evaluating the Bible's statements in the light of archaeological finds. When we do, we find that the New Testament writings are historically accurate.[1]

The implications are rather startling. We know that Jesus claimed to be God, and this then leaves us with very few options.

C. S. Lewis in *Mere Christianity* commented:

> I am trying here to prevent anyone saying the really foolish thing that people often say about Him: "I'm ready to accept Jesus as a great moral teacher, but I don't accept His claim to be God." That is the one thing we must not say. A man who was merely a man and said the sort of things Jesus said would not be a great moral teacher. He would either be a lunatic—on a level with the man who says he is a poached egg—or else he would be the Devil of Hell. You must make your choice. Either this man was, and is, the

Son of God: or else a madman or something worse. You can shut Him up for a fool, you can spit at Him and kill Him as a demon; or you can fall at His feet and call Him Lord and God. But let us not come with any patronising nonsense about His being a great human teacher. He has not left that open to us. He did not intend to.[2]

As Jon Buell and Quentin Hyder state in their book *Jesus: God, Ghost, or Guru?* the only reasonable option in the light of the large amount of data available is that Jesus was and is God[3] and therefore He Himself is the verification of all that He has said and of all that the Bible declares—also concerning matters of what lies beyond death.

Is There Life After Death?

In John 3:12 Jesus said, "I have spoken to you of earthly things and you do not believe; how then will you believe if I speak of heavenly things?" The implication is that if we doubt what Jesus said about empirical data, which we can verify, we will never believe what He says about supernatural matters, which we cannot verify.

This point has an important bearing on our question concerning afterlife experiences. The best testimony does not come from those who have momentarily left their bodies, but rather from the One who stepped out of eternity into time. God's revelation is of much greater value than the subjective experiences of those with near-death experiences.

So what is the truth about life after death? Jesus definitely taught that there is a life after death. He taught that His followers would have eternal life (Matt. 19:29; 25:46; Mark 10:30; John 12:25). Others confirm His teaching. John the Baptist taught it (John 3:36). The apostle Paul wrote about the hope of eternal life (Titus 1:2). John the apostle did so too (1 John 2:25).

These claims were not presented as a new revelation but rather as a development and expansion of the claims made in the Old Testament. This was made especially clear on one of the occasions when Jesus was confronted by the Saducees. Though they did not believe in life after death, they nevertheless questioned Him concerning the afterlife (Matt. 22:23–32; Mark 12:18–27; Luke 20:27–38). In order to give them an answer they would accept, He needed to make a case for eternal life from one of the first five Books of the Bible, since they accepted only those books as inspired.

Jesus turned to Exodus to prove His point. In Exodus 3:6, God said to Moses, "I am the God of Abraham, the God of Isaac, and the God of Jacob." Since all three of these men had been dead for over four hundred years in Moses' day, the use of the present tense would make sense only if they were still alive in some other state after death. With that Jesus concluded, "He is not the God of the dead, but of the living, for to him all are alive" (Luke 20:38).

Perhaps the greatest lesson Jesus used to teach that we will live after death was the resurrection of his friend Lazarus. He first taught Martha that He was the resurrection and the life (John 11:25). Then He proved it by raising Lazarus from the grave after he had been dead for four days. To any Jew this would be proof that though he was dead physically, Lazarus had continued to exist spiritually until Jesus brought him back to life.

Not only does the Bible teach that there is life after death, it tells us a great deal about what the afterlife is like. How much do the afterlife experiences of our day correlate with the biblical data? Let us begin by noting that most OBEs are very pleasant in nature. But the story of the rich man and Lazarus teaches us that there are two very different types of experience. Why this difference?

Pleasant Experiences

It should not be too surprising that many people report pleasant out-of-the-body experiences. The Bible teaches that God is love (1 John 4:16) and is not willing that anyone should perish (2 Peter 3:9). We should, however, be disturbed if evil men had the same experience as good men. If a pleasant experience awaits everyone from the saint to Adolf Hitler and Ghengis Khan, then the idea of justice in the world is destroyed. But we would be equally disturbed if all of the pleasant experiences were merely counterfeits.

There is good reason to believe that many pleasant out-of-the-body experiences are genuine. Many of those reported by Christians correlate with the biblical accounts. They were not any "more dead" than others, but in this intermediate state they may have seen what the Bible describes.

People working in the helping professions (the clergy, medical personnel) often report that Christians who are dying have a joyful expression on their faces. As Leslie Weatherhead notes, dying people sometimes see into the next life.

> I have seen a number of people die, and I have made enquiries of nurses and doctors. You'll appreciate that most people die following a state of unconsciousness. Either they are in a coma or are drugged. But I have sat at the bedside of a man who was dying and conscious to the end. He gripped my hand and I must have gripped his more tightly than I thought I was doing, for he said, "Don't hold me back. I can see through the gates. It's marvelous."[4]

Such a testimony is not unusual. History is filled with cases of Christian men and women who have seen a glimpse of the afterlife before they died. One well-known case comes from the biography of Dwight L. Moody, the famous evangelist who died shortly before the turn of the century.

While he was on his deathbed, he had just such an experience and then regained consciousness. He said, "I went to the gate of heaven. Why, it was so wonderful. And I saw the children!" After a brief conversation, he died with serenity and expectation.[5]

Though there are many accounts in history of such deathbed Christian visions, many modern near-death accounts have also been reported. When we eliminate those that might have physiological, psychological, and pharmacological causes, there are still some that correlate with biblical descriptions of the afterlife.

One such example comes from an experience of a seventy-year-old accountant whose report Dr. Maurice Rawlings tape-recorded. It is used here by permission.

They were rushing me from the emergency room to the intensive care unit because of my chest pain. They told me it was a heart attack. In the elevator, I felt my heart stop and I stopped breathing and I thought, "This is it."

The next thing I remember was looking down on my body in the intensive care unit. I don't know how I got there, but they were working on me. There was this young doctor in a white coat and two nurses and a black fellow in a white uniform and he was doing most of the work on me. This black fellow was shoving down on my chest and someone else was breathing for me and they were yelling to "get this and get that!"

I learned later that this black fellow was a male nurse on the ward. I had never seen him before. I even remember the black bow tie he was wearing.

Next thing I remember was going through this dark passage. I didn't touch any of the walls. I emerged out into an open field and was walking toward a big white wall which was very long. It has three steps leading up to a doorway in the wall. On a landing above the stairs sat a man clothed in a robe that was dazzling white and glowing. His face had a glowing radiance also. He was looking down into a big book, studying.

As I approached Him I felt a great reverence and I asked him, "Are you Jesus?"

He said, "No, you will find Jesus and your loved ones beyond the door." After he looked in his book he said, "You may go through."

And then I walked through the door, and saw on the other side this beautiful, brilliantly lit city, reflecting what seemed to be the sun's rays. It was all made of gold or some shiny metal with domes and steeples in beautiful array, and the streets were shining, not quite like marble but made of something I have never seen before. There were many people all dressed in glowing white robes with radiant faces. They looked beautiful. The air smelled so fresh. I have never smelled anything like it.

There was a background of music that was beautiful, heavenly music, and I saw two figures walking toward me and I immediately recognized them. They were my mother and father; both had died years ago. My mother was an amputee and yet that leg was now restored! She was walking on two legs!

I said to my mother, "You and father are beautiful."

And they said to me, "You have the same radiance and you are also beautiful."

As we walked along together to find Jesus, I noticed there was one building larger than all of the others. It looked like a football stadium with an open end to the building where a blinding light radiated from it. I tried to look up at the light but couldn't. It was too brilliant. Many people seemed to be bowed in front of this building in adoration and prayer.

I said to my parents, "What is that?"

They said, "In there is God."

I will never forget it. I have never seen anything like it. We walked on as they were taking to me to see Jesus and we passed many people. All of them were happy. I have never felt such a sense of well-being.

As we approached the place where Jesus was located, I suddenly felt this tremendous surge of electricity through my body as if someone had hit me in the chest. My body arched upward as they were defibrillating my heart. I had been restored to my former life! But I was not too happy to come back. However, I knew I had been sent back to tell others about this experience. I plan to dedicate the rest of my life to telling anyone who will listen![6]

Experiences like this one are interesting because they correlate with biblical descriptions.

Others tell of being transported by angels and they describe a heavenly city in essentially the same terms as those found in the Book of Revelation in the Bible. Often these descriptions come from those who were not previously familiar with that part of the Bible.[7]

Our hope for eternal life, however, is not in this experience but rather in the person of Jesus Christ. Such experiences are interesting and perhaps genuine but not a sufficient basis for faith. In many cases, as we shall now see, pleasant experiences may actually be pleasant memories. Not all trips are pleasant trips.

Unpleasant Experiences

In his book *Life After Life*, Raymond Moody came to the following conclusion:

> Through all of my research, however, I have not heard a single reference to a heaven or a hell anything like the customary picture to which we are exposed in this society. Indeed, many persons have stressed how unlike their experiences were to what they had been led to expect in the course of their religious training.[8]

Throughout his first book Dr. Moody continually noted that the experiences of those who had near-death encounters were routinely positive and pleasant. Never was there any mention of unpleasant experiences or visions of hell.

In time other people began to follow with similar claims. After talking to over one hundred patients, Kenneth Ring, a psychology professor at the University of Connecticut, states: "Nobody reported to me experiencing images of hell."[9] In Florida, Dr. Michael Sabom (now at Emory University) and Sarah Kreutziger also were collecting near-death accounts. After his research, Sabom "became convinced that these experiences are very real to the persons and are uniformly pleasant."[10]

These people began to attract the attention of the medical profession because they published their conclusions in medical journals like the *Journal of the Florida Medical Association*[11] and *The New England Journal of Medicine*.[12] They reported that these people had experienced "a tremendous sense of calm and peace . . . in this detached state. Some then pass into a different environment consistently described as being filled with love, beauty and peace."[13]

But despite such reports, it is nevertheless true that patients occasionally return with very unpleasant experiences. Some return in shock or in stark terror. They have indeed had a very negative vision and are terrified to encounter death again.

If there are such negative experiences, one might ask why they have not been reported. There are probably four major reasons. First, negative experiences are relatively rare and most of the initial studies were made of a small sample of people. For example, when Raymond Moody did his work for his first book, he found no references to heaven or hell. But, in his later book *Reflections on Life After Life,* he changed his earlier conclusions.

> I stated in *Life After Life* that I had not found any cases in which a "heaven"—at least in a certain traditional portrayal of that place—was described. However, I have now talked with numerous individuals who tell with remarkable consistency of catching glimpses of other realms of being which may be termed "heavenly." It is interesting to me that in several accounts a single phrase—"a city of light"—occurs. In this and several other respects the imagery in which these scenes are described seems to be reminiscent of what is found in *The Bible*.[14]

When his sample size increased, not only did he find references to a pleasant image like heaven, but he also found unpleasant experiences.

139

Several people have reported to me that at some point they glimpsed other beings who seemed to be "trapped" in an apparently most unfortunate state of existence. Those who described seeing these confused beings are in agreement on several points.[15]

One woman described people who "seemed to shuffle, as someone would on a chain gang" and had "this absolute, crushed, hopeless demeanor."[16] She said she went to a world where there were only shades and tones of gray, and what she saw was quite depressing.

A second reason people do not report negative experiences is that they are sometimes ignored as anomalous. For example, the author of *Deathbed Observations by Physicians and Nurses* says:

In our sample we find something along traditional lines in this case: "The patient had a horrified expression, turned his head in all directions and said, 'Hell, Hell, all I see is Hell.'" Another had the terrifying feeling of being burned alive. These are only two cases in our collection to strike a distressing, emotional note—a small minority indeed when compared with the number reporting peace and beauty.[17]

Even in his later study of deathbed experiences in America and India, he found "a strong percentage—18 percent—who felt very upset. They had fearful visions and didn't want to go. It was as if soldiers came to take prisoners—a real fear reaction."[18]

But even when such negative experiences are found, they are rarely reported. The reports generally devote little space to them, and popular reports that appear in newsmagazines or newspapers often even omit any reference to them. The overall effect is that the average person thinks *all* afterlife experiences are positive.

A third reason that few unpleasant experiences are reported may be the fact that a very large majority of the afterlife experiences are of short duration. The result is that there would not be sufficient time for an entire situation to unfold. An OBE might begin with a pleasant feeling of transcendence and never progress to the place where negative images might arise. This is quite reasonable in the light of biblical teachings that a final judgment will occur in the future. It would then very well be possible that while a person was in such an intermediate state he would have few negative experiences.

Finally, people are often interviewed long after the experiences. This allows for the possibility of embellishment and the suppression of negative aspects of the experience.

In reviewing these cases, Moody noticed that there was evidence of possible suppression:

> Finally, it is quite possible that in many cases the reverse of embellishment had taken place. What psychiatrists call "suppression" is a mental mechanism whereby a conscious effort is made to control undesired memories, feelings, or thoughts, or to conceal them from awareness. On numerous occasions in the course of interviews, persons have made remarks which are strongly indicative that suppression has occurred.[19]

If suppression does indeed occur, the best possible way to get accurate reporting is to interview patients shortly after they have been resuscitated.

In *Human Personality and Its Survival of Bodily Death*, Dr. W. H. Myers concurs:

> It is possible that we might learn much upon questioning dying persons on their awakening from some comatose condition, as to their memory of any dream or visions during this state. If there has in fact been any such experience, it should be at once recorded, as it will probably fade rapidly from the patient's supraliminal memory, even if he does not die directly afterwards.[20]

When this is done, the percentage of negative experiences increases. We do not know whether they are suppressed by some psychological mechanism or by a spiritual force. But what is certain is that negative experiences are usually forgotten in a very short period of time.

Dr. Maurice Rawlings in *Beyond Death's Door* reports one such instance.[21] He recounts an experience he had when a patient dropped dead to the floor. In the midst of CPR (cardiopulmonary resuscitation) the patient began to scream that he was in hell. He had a terrified look, his pupils were dilated, he was perspiring and trembling, and his hair was "on end."

Two days later he returned to interview his patient to find out what he saw in hell. By that time his patient knew nothing about a trip to hell. The experiences were probably so frightening that his conscious mind could not cope with them.

Even though a great number of negative experiences have not been reported, there are some that parallel a traditional view of hell. The following account related by Thomas Welch occurred while he was working as an engineer's helper for the Bridal Veil Lumber Company. It is reprinted here by permission.

> I went out on the trestle to straighten out some timbers which were crossed and not moving on a conveyor. Suddenly I fell off the trestle and tumbled down between the timbers and into the pond, which was ten feet deep. An engineer sitting in the cab of his locomotive unloading logs into the pond saw me fall. I landed on my head on the first beam thirty feet down, and then tumbled from one beam to another until I fell into the water and disappeared from his view.
>
> There were seventy men working in and around the mill at that time. The mill was shut down then and every available man was called to search for my body, according to the testimonies of these men. The search went on for forty-five minutes to one hour before I was finally found by M. J. H. Gunderson, who has written his own account of this to verify the facts of this testimony.
>
> I was dead as far as this world is concerned. But I was alive in another world. There was no lost time. I learned more in that hour out of the body than I could ever learn while in this body. All I

could remember is falling over the edge of the trestle. The locomotive engineer watched me go all the way down into the water.

The next thing I knew I was standing near a shoreline of a great ocean of fire. It happened to be what the Bible says it is in Revelation 21:8: ". . . the lake which burneth with fire and brimstone." This is the most awesome sight one could ever see this side of the final judgment.

I remember more clearly than any other thing that has ever happened to me in my lifetime every detail of every moment, what I saw and what happened during that hour I was gone from this world. I was standing some distance from this burning, turbulent, rolling mass of blue fire. As far as my eyes could see it was just the same. A lake of fire and brimstone. There was nobody in it. I was not in it. I saw other people whom I had known that had died when I was thirteen. Another was a boy I had gone to school with who had died from cancer of the jaw that had started with an infected tooth while he was just a young lad. He was two years older than I. We recognized each other, even though we did not speak. They, too, were looking and seemed to be perplexed and in deep thought, as though they could not believe what they saw. Their expressions were those of bewilderment and confusion.

The scene was so awesome that words simply fail. There is no way to describe it except to say we were eye witnesses now to the final judgment. There is no way to escape, no way out. You don't even try to look for one. This is the prison out of which no one can escape except by Divine intervention. I said to myself in an audible voice, "If I had known about this I would have done anything that was required of me to escape coming to a place like this." But I had not known.

As these thoughts were racing through my mind, I saw another man coming by in front of us. I knew immediately who He was. He had a strong, kind, compassionate face, composed and unafraid, Master of all He saw. It was Jesus Himself.

A great hope took hold of me and I knew the answer to my problem was this great and wonderful Person who was moving by me in this prison of lost, confused judgment-bound souls. I did not do anything to attract His attention. I said again to myself, "If He would only look my way and see me, He could rescue me from this place because He would know what to do." He passed on by and it seemed as though He would not look my way, but just before He passed out of sight He turned His head and looked directly at me. That is all it took. His look was enough.

In seconds I was back entering into my body again. It was like coming in through the door of a house. I could hear the Brockes (the people I was staying with) praying minutes before I could open my eyes or say anything. I could hear and I understood what was going on. Then suddenly life came into my body and I opened my eyes and spoke to them.[22]

What we can see from all of this investigation is that these afterlife experiences often do correlate with biblical teaching on life after death. Despite the initial conclusions of many researchers that there was no correlation, there are many very striking similarities. But there are many things that we cannot discover about the life beyond death by experience. This information must come from revelation.

In the next chapter, we will look at what the Bible teaches about the life that awaits each of us at death. We will look at what life after death is really like and see how each of us can be sure of the destiny that awaits us on the other side of the grave.

EIGHT

OUR LIVES
BEYOND
DEATH

People have always wondered what life after death might be like. The *Tibetan Book of the Dead (Bardo Thödol)* describes a series of bardos (or stages) through which a person must pass in the next life. The Egyptians prepared for the afterlife and all that it contained through many physical countermeasures described in the *Egyptian Book of the Dead (Pert Em Hru)*. Spells, incantations, hymns, and prayers were all part of the process of crossing the river Styx.

The Greeks had visions of youths running through Elysian fields. In the Middle Ages people looked forward eagerly to the beauty and serenity of heaven. They actually welcomed death rather than dreading it and they spoke about the art of dying in order to help others anticipate and prepare for their next life.

In modern times man has not been sure that there is life after death. Biology tells him he dies like any other animal. Psychology tells him he is little more than a preprogrammed machine. Therefore, he wonders whether there really is a life after death. T. S. Eliot speaks for him:

We are the hollow men
We are the stuffed men
  Leaning together
  Head piece filled with straw.

    . . . .

This is the way the world ends,
Not with a bang but a whimper.[1]

Life for many today does not end with a bang and a promise of life beyond the grave. It ends with a whimper and they expect nothing more. As Peggy Lee sang many years ago, "Is that all there is?" For many today the answer is yes.

On the other hand, many people have been unwilling to accept this stark conclusion. They continue to look for ways to confirm the existence of an afterlife and find out what it is like. The intense interest on the part of many investigators in OBEs to determine the nature of the afterlife is proof of their search. Robert Monroe has said that some of the people he sent on OBEs while they were alive have come back to tell him that life is much the same in the afterlife as it is in this one.[2] Mediums who supposedly contact the dead also report that life on the other side of the grave is similar to this life.

But how do we really know what is true? We have already seen that OBE reports and medium contacts are not a sufficient basis for trust. They are subjective and nonverifiable.

In contrast, the Bible claims to give reliable information of the afterlife. It claims to be God's revelation. As we have evaluated it, we have found it worthy of a faith commitment. What does the Bible say about our lives beyond death?

Immortality and Eternal Life

I pointed out in chapter 7 that the Bible promises life after death to those who believe in Jesus Christ. It is the clear teaching of both the Old and New Testaments. But if that is true, we might wonder why so many cultures and societies have some form of belief in life after death. As Cicero so memorably put it, "There is in the minds of men, I know not how, a certain presage, as it were, of a future existence; and this takes deepest root in the greatest geniuses and the most exalted souls."[3]

The reason for this phenomenon can be found in Ecclesiastes 3:11. God has set eternity in the heart of every person so that his soul reaches out for eternal life. Moreover, we are taught in Romans 1:18–19 that man knows in his heart there is a God, though that truth may be suppressed. Therefore it is not surprising that there are many cultures around the world that, having once been familiar with the Bible, but now being so no longer, still espouse similar views of the afterlife.

Because each of us has a heart that is longing for immortality, it is important that we distinguish between what may be our personal speculation and what is actually taught in the Bible. People have many views of immortality, and it is crucial that on such an important topic we separate speculation from revelation.

In casual conversation when we talk about immortality, we are often talking about a Greek concept rather than a biblical one. Plato was the first to incorporate the idea of immortality into a logical and systematic pattern. In his dialogue *Phaedo*, he introduces his proofs for immortality in the final scene of Socrates' life.

Plato argues that death is something that should be accepted since it allows the soul to be released from the body. Only the body is corruptible and subject to death. Since he saw the soul as immortal, he defined death as normal, natural, and necessary to release the soul from its prison, the body, which he said was evil.

The teaching of the New Testament is quite different.

First, death is not normal. It is an abnormal feature of life on this earth caused by the fall of man (Gen. 3:19; Rom. 5:12). When Jesus saw death, He indicated that He felt it was abnormal and worthy of grief (John 11:33). Paul said that "the last enemy to be destroyed is death" (1 Cor. 15:26).

Second, there is almost no mention of immortality in the Bible. The literal translation of *immortality* is "deathlessness." Using this definition, only one person is truly immortal, and that is God. In this sense 1 Timothy 6:16 says that God "alone is immortal." But when the word is used in other contexts, it has a different meaning.

For example, in 2 Timothy 1:10, Jesus is said to have "destroyed death and . . . brought life and immortality to light through the gospel." Jesus has defeated eternal death for those who believe in Him. Eternal life is possible for the believer because spiritual death has been defeated. A final victory is won at the time of the physical death of the believer.

Yet despite these differences between Greek and Christian thought, the Greek concept of immortality became part of the Christian theology. Augustine's synthesis of the philosophy of Plato with Christianity and other forms of Neo-Platonism have become an integral part of our contemporary concept of immortality.*

In order to clairfy these different concepts of immortality, let us look briefly at four fundamental differences between the Greek and the biblical views of immortality. First, Greek phiilosophers after the time of Plato taught that all men were immortal. The Bible teaches that only God is immortal. It

---

*Briefly, we can trace this influence from such early church theologians as Clement of Alexandria, Origen, and Augustine of Hippo through the Lateran Council of 1512 to the Protestant reformers who incorporated a Greek doctrine of immortality into their confessions of faith in the seventeenth century.

In the Catholic church, Thomas Aquinas was influenced by the similar outlook of Aristotle. He suggested that some souls spent some time in heaven waiting for their resurrection but did not resolve how sinful souls could go to heaven.

adds that only believers in Jesus Christ have eternal life.

Second, the Greeks conceived of immortality as the endless existence of the soul. The Bible on the other hand, speaks of the resurrection of the "body." Immediately at death the soul, and later the glorified body of the believer, receive eternal blessings in heaven. The biblical view of the body is very different from the Greek view. The body is not a mere castoff or a dispensible commodity. The believer's body is described as the temple of the living God (2 Cor. 6:16) that will for a short time be shed. Paul compares death to the tearing down of a tent (2 Cor. 5:1). Later, the body will be raised from the dead according to the promises of both the Old Testament (Dan. 12:2) and the New Testament (John 5:28; Rev. 20:12).

Third, the purpose of eternal life differs. The Greeks believed that everyone would be immortal. The Bible says that eternal life is a gift from God given to those who believe in His Son, Jesus Christ. The believer's new body is no longer a temporal, earthly dwelling but rather an eternal, spiritual one (1 Cor. 15:44; 2 Cor. 5:1).

Finally, the Greeks could only speculate that man might be immortal. While waiting to drink the hemlock that produced his death, Socrates said, "I would not positively assert that I shall join the company of those good men who have already departed from this life, but I cherish a good hope."[4] The biblical hope of immortality is very different. This hope is not an uncertain hope. It is hope based on the assurance of God's promise that the believer will live forever. There are various definitions for the different words in the Bible we translate as "hope," but all of them imply assurance and certainty. They speak of a hope that gives new strength, a hope that gives assurance, and a hope that inspires trust.[5] Each has assurance and is a certain hope.

It is not, however, the assurance of eternal life that makes Christianity unique. The crucial difference is the claim of resurrection. Christianity does not offer one merely a continued, conscious existence as a disembodied soul. It offers the resurrection of the body to eternal life.

The basis for this belief is the resurrection of Jesus Christ. The resurrection is the very foundation of Christianity. The Bible promises the believer that his mortal body will receive life (Rom. 8:11). The one who raised Jesus from death will also resurrect the believer in the future (2 Cor. 4:14).

The message about Jesus' resurrection is the fundamental message of the New Testament. The apostle Paul in his letter to the church in Corinth said that "if Christ has not been raised, your faith is futile" and those "who have fallen asleep in Christ are lost" (1 Cor. 15:17–18).

Christianity risks its truth claim on this one historical event. Either it is true and there is eternal life or it is not and the Christian's faith is futile (1 Cor. 15:17). No other religious founder ever rose from the grave. If Christ's resurrection actually occurred, it is not only a unique event but also a spectacular event worthy of our commitment. It would not be a resuscitation after a few minutes but rather a resurrection after three days.

Resurrection not Resuscitation

In the previous chapter we looked at the historical evidence for the life and ministry of Jesus while He was on the earth. Now let us use these same reliable historical sources and focus on one particular event: His resurrection.

Since the resurrection of Jesus is the very cornerstone of Christianity, there are many books and articles written on the subject. Rather than give a complete and detailed account of the events and the historical evidence, let us briefly survey the evidence that has convinced so many skeptics that Jesus rose from the grave.

Few would deny the basic historical facts surrounding the

birth and sudden growth of Christianity. But it is this sudden growth that must be explained if one does *not* believe in the resurrection of Jesus. When Jesus was crucified, the disciples were afraid and scattered throughout the land. Yet within weeks of that event they were once again together and preaching with one accord that Jesus rose from the grave. The Roman Empire was upset by "these men who have caused trouble all over the world" (Acts 17:6). They went out and created a stir wherever they went because they preached the unpopular message that Jesus rose from the grave.

Aside from the historical evidence of the growth of Christianity there is other, more direct, evidence of the Resurrection. Before the Resurrection, the following six events took place: (1) Jesus had died (John 19:31–37); (2) He was removed from the cross and buried according to Jewish custom (John 19:40); (3) He was placed in a rock tomb (Matt. 27:60; John 19:41–42); (4) a very large stone was laid against the entrance of the tomb (Matt. 27:60; Mark 16:4; Luke 24:2; John 20:1); (5) a Roman guard unit was placed on guard at the tomb (Matt. 27:62–66); and (6) all the disciples had fled except John and the women (Mark 14:50; John 19:25–27).

The postresurrection scene is very different. First, the tomb was empty except for the graveclothes, which were still intact (John 20:1–10). Second, the stone had been rolled away from the tomb (Mark 16:1–4), something the women who came early could not have done. Third, the women (Matt. 28:9–10; Mark 16:9–11; John 20:13–18), the disciples (Matt. 28:16–20; Mark 16:12–20; Luke 24:13–53; John 20:19–31), and more than five-hundred other witnesses (1 Cor. 15:6) saw Him after His resurrection. This evidence had led many scholars to the conclusion that the only logical option is that Jesus actually arose from the grave.[6]

Because Jesus rose from the grave, we can be sure that if we place our faith in Him He will give us eternal life. He is the

151

Master over death, and we can trust in Him. Moreover, the Resurrection establishes His credibility as an authority on the subject of the afterlife. We do not have to trust in speculation on the subject of life after death. Instead, we can listen to the One who has seen both sides of death. He can tell us what it will be like on the other side of death.

Our Bodies After Death

What will our bodies be like in the afterlife? This is one question we can answer simply by examining the eyewitness accounts of Jesus after His resurrection. If we will be raised like Him, then our bodies will be like His.

One of the striking features of the postresurrection accounts concerning Jesus is that often He was not recognized. There must have been some changes in His appearance because His closest friends mistook Him for someone else. Mary thought He was a gardener when she saw Him (John 20:15). Two of His disciples walked with Him to the town of Emmaus and did not recognize Him until He broke bread with them (Luke 24:30–31). Even the disciples who were fishing did not recognize Him on the shore until He had performed a miracle (John 21:1–13).

Though they did not always recognize Him initially, there were characteristics that were the same. Mary responded to His words, the disciples at Emmaus to His mannerisms, and His other disciples to His miracles. We also see that when Moses and Elijah appeared on the Mount of Transfiguration, though they had been dead for centuries, the disciples recognized them (Matt. 17:1–13). Enough of their form was recognizable to the disciples that they could identify them.

But it was not just His outward features that had changed. In His postresurrection appearances Jesus was different also in other ways. He had a body and was not simply a ghost or a spirit (Luke 24:38–39), since He could be touched and He

152

could eat a meal or fish. His disciples could see that He had a body of flesh and bones (Luke 24:39–43).

But though He had a body, it was a very different one from the body He had before His resurrection. He was able to enter rooms whose doors were locked (John 20:19). He was also apparently able to appear in places at will without having to use the normal means of travel, and He was later taken up into the air on the Mount of Ascension (Acts 1:9). In His post-resurrection state He transcended space and time but until His ascension He retained the ability to reenter it at will.

In transcending the physical limitations of His preresurrection body, Jesus also transcended the effects of death. Paul tells us that because God raised Jesus from the dead, "death no longer has mastery over him" (Rom. 6:9). He no longer had a mortal body, and so He was no longer subject to sickness, disease, or death.

The same can be true for us. The believer is promised the same conscious experience after death that was His. Our experience will be different. But it will also be the same. We will have a new body, but we will still be basically the same. This was best communicated by Dr. Donald MacKay of Keele University when he said:

> It is not as disembodied spirits that God promises us eternal life, but as personalities expressed in a new kind of body—what the apostle Paul calls a "spiritual body." Just as a message is still the same message, whether it's spoken in words or flashed in Morse code, so, according to the Bible, we shall be the same persons, whatever the material form in which our personalities may be expressed.[7]

The Bible also tells us that the believer will rest from his labor (Rev. 14:13), which also includes his toil, sorrow, pain, and sin. He will work, but in God's service (Matt. 25:21).

His senses will also be active. Revelation 22:4 says that believers will see Christ's face, and different references to music imply that they will hear. The believer will also inherit full intellectual powers, including the wisdom of the universe (1 Cor. 13:12).

It is not difficult to see why the New Testament writers spoke of the joy of life after death. The world that awaited them was so shining and bright that this world was dull by comparison. Christians are to be with Jesus and reign with Him and share all that He has (Rev. 3:12, 21). No wonder they could speak of the joy of death.

The Joy of Death

One of the most significant features about the change in the attitude of the disciples after the resurrection of Jesus is the fact that they never again used the word *death* when they talked about the end of a Christian's life. Instead, they expected "to be at home with the Lord," "to depart and be with Christ," "to sleep in Jesus," or to be "forever with the Lord." Death is not the end. Rather it inaugurates a time of great joy. The early Christians saw death not as loss but as gain.

It is important that we get an accurate perspective of this fact of faith since it is foundational to a Christian perspective of grief. In 1 Thessalonians 4:13, the Christian is told not "to grieve like the rest of the men, who have no hope." This does not mean that the Christian is not to grieve at all. Jesus wept at the tomb of Lazarus before He raised him from the dead (John 11:33). His expression of emotions there refuted for all time the macho myth that tears are only for the weak.

The verse actually says that Christians are not to grieve as others do. This is because they have the firm conviction that for those who believe a glorious fate awaits on the other side of the grave. They know that to be at home in the body is to be away from the Lord (2 Cor. 5:6) but that to be absent from the body is to be at home with the Lord (2 Cor. 5:8). Paul wrote to the Philippian church that he was torn between the two options: to depart and to be with Christ or to continue to remain and minister here on earth (Phil. 1:21–26). The former, he felt, was better.

Such an attitude is crucial to the development of a Christian attitude toward death. Death may bring separation and the sorrow that comes from saying good-bye, but it also brings the joyful culmination of a life that precedes a glorious eternal life for the believer. Those who are left behind can be comforted by the fact that their departed loved one is now living the most abundant life possible.

The New Testament writers used two different figures of speech to illustrate their belief in the abundance of the next life.[8] The first is that of *departure* (*exodus*, sometimes figurative for "decease"). When Jesus was on the Mount of Transfiguration, the subject of conversation was His "departure" (Luke 9:31). Later in the New Testament Peter uses the same word to speak of his own death (2 Peter 1:15). The word is the same one used in Hebrews 11:22 to describe the exodus of the children of Israel from Egypt to the Promised Land. Hence the image that is being described of death is that it is something higher and more desirable. At death we can throw off the shackles of this life as the Jews did in Egypt and come into the Promised Land of eternal life as they did when they entered the Land flowing with milk and honey (Exod. 3:8, 17; 13:5; 33:3). Death is a deliverance from slavery to freedom.

The second figure of speech is that of *setting sail*. Paul told Timothy that "the time has come for my departure" (2 Tim. 4:6). The word for "departure" is a nautical term referring to a ship getting ready to set sail. The image is again one of abundance and joy. A ship getting ready to set sail has been tied to the dock and all preparations were made in the midst of the bustle and mess of the dock. Often foul smells, rats, and filth are part of the preparations. But once the ship is set loose,

155

it is free to sail in the beauty of the seas and the power of the wind. It is doing what it was made to do. The sea is the home of the ship, just as the next life is our true home. But just as a ship must spend time at the docks, we must spend our time in this life until we are set loose. We are preparing for the time when we cast off into the bright seas of eternity.

The next life represents gain for the believer. As Paul says, "For me to live is Christ, and to die is gain" (Phil. 1:21). Death is gain in many ways.[9] First, we exchange time for eternity. In this life, we are locked into time; we suffer toils, trials, and disappointments; and we have only limited knowledge. In the next life, we will be in eternity with a life of joy, abundance, and full knowledge. As Paul says, "Now we see but a poor reflection; then we shall see face to face. Now I know in part; then I shall know fully, even as I am fully known" (1 Cor. 13:12).

Death is also a gain in that it delivers us from bondage. When a person commits his life to Jesus Christ, he is born again (John 3:3). Jesus died for man's sins (Rom. 5:8) so that if we receive Him (John 1:12) and believe in Him, we will inherit eternal life (John 3:16) and become new creatures (2 Cor. 6:2). But though the process of regeneration produces changes in the life and state of the believer, it does not remove such results of the fall of man as physical death. Our hearts are still troubled with evil (Matt. 15:19) and await the future and final cure (Jer. 17:9; Rom. 7:18). The flesh still wars against the spirit (Gal. 5:17).

Regeneration does not end that war. It merely provides the believer with a means of victory. His old nature is broken so that through the power of God he can put it off (Eph. 4:22), make it his slave (1 Cor. 9:27), consider it dead (Rom. 6:11), and put it to death (Col. 3:5). Because a believer still lives in the flesh (Gal. 2:20), he cannot experience complete deliverance from the effects of sin until the day he dies. This is when total deliverance from sin and the limitations of life is experienced.

Death is gain because it brings the believer into full and complete fellowship with God. When we sinned, we fell short of the glory of God (Rom. 3:23). Sin stands as a barrier between us and God. Even after we commit ourselves to Jesus Christ, we do not have as close and intimate a fellowship with God as we will in the next life. The same is true of our fellowship with others. Now we are encumbered by the cares of this world and are limited in knowledge, communication, and compassion. In the next, these barriers will no longer exist.

In brief, death can be a joyful experience. It is like an exodus or departure for the Promised Land. And it brings gain in many ways. What is it like? Where does the believer go at death and what does he experience?

Heaven

When we read the Bible, we can very easily be confused as to what awaits the believer after death. Much of this confusion is a confusion of terms. For example, in the Old Testament the word *sheol* may be translated "grave," "Hades," or "hell" and lead many to think that Old Testament believers were not in heaven or were not aware of heaven. This confusion stems from the fact that the Hebrew language had only the one broad word to describe the abode of those who died. Thus in the story of the rich man and Lazarus (Luke 16:19–31) both went to Hades (the most common word in the Greek language as well).

When speaking of the place for the spirits of believers, early Christians often used the term *Abraham's bosom*—also used for Lazarus's final resting place (Luke 16:22). This was separated by a great chasm from the place of the wicked where the rich man was (Luke 16:23, 26).

It may seem confusing when we note how many different

157

terms are used for the resting place of the righteous. For example, Jesus told the dying thief on the cross: "Today you will be with me in paradise" (Luke 23:43). Paul talks about his "desire to depart and be with Christ" (Phil. 1:23). When he was about to be stoned, Stephen looked up and saw "Jesus standing at the right hand of God" (Acts 7:55). And Jesus told His disciples there were many "rooms" in His "Father's house" and that He was going to prepare a "place" for them (John 14:2–3).

Actually, however, there is no confusion. The Bible simply uses different terms to describe the same location. It may be called heaven, paradise, or the Father's house and yet be the same place. In fact, Paul refers to a man who was caught up to the third heaven (2 Cor. 12:2) in a possible out-of-body experience. Then later he calls the place paradise (2 Cor. 12:4). Thus he uses two different terms to refer to the same place.

Second, different terms are used because of what Jesus Christ did on the cross. Before His death and ascension the righteous went to paradise to wait for His coming. After His ascension the believer goes to be with Him immediately at death. Thus in the story of the rich man and Lazarus (Luke 16:19–31) the abode of the believer was Abraham's bosom. But after the death and ascension of Jesus the believer no longer has to pass through the portals of Hades, but instead goes immediately to be with Him.

While we are on this concept, it would be very good to clear up a misconception that some have about the state of the believer after death. Some believe that when we die, we will go into a sleep (often called soul sleep) and await the call of the Lord in the resurrection of the body.

The idea of soul sleep has a long history. Early in the history of the Christian church, there was a group of believers in Arabia who believed in the sleep of the soul. Various sects have held this belief through the centuries. By the time of the

Reformation, Calvin refuted it in his treatise *Psychopannychia*, but there are still some today who would argue that the Bible teaches soul sleep.

What does the Bible teach? There are passages in the Old Testament that speak of death as sleep (Gen. 47:30; Deut. 31:16; 2 Sam. 7:12; 2 Chron. 33:20). In the New Testament, the Greek word for "sleep" is *koimaomai*, which occurs eighteen times. In fourteen of those cases sleep means death (e.g., Matt. 27:52; Luke 8:52; John 11:11–13; Acts 7:60; 1 Cor. 7:39; 15:6, 18; 1 Thess. 4:13).

But though death may be called sleep, there is no indication that it is the soul that sleeps. It is just as likely that these verses are only emphasizing that the body sleeps. This would be in accord with other verses that state that the body ceases from its labor (Rev. 14:13) but do not make any such statement about the soul. The body may indeed "sleep" as it loses consciousness, but the soul is present with the Lord (2 Cor. 5:8).

This interpretation is supported by verses that indicate that the souls of believers are awake after death. Lazarus was immediately carried to Abraham's bosom (Luke 16:20) and did not pass through soul sleep. What the believer experiences in heaven does not compare with life on earth (Rom. 8:18), because he is immediately in the presence of Christ (Phil. 1:23; 2 Cor. 5:8). There is no indication of any span of time in these verses. Rather, "to be away from the body" is to be "at home with the Lord" (2 Cor. 5:8).

Belief in soul sleep cannot be supported from the Bible unless we consider only those verses that refer to death as sleep. Other verses clearly indicating that the souls of believers are awake argues against such a notion. While on the cross, Jesus did not promise the repentant thief a life in heaven at some later date. Instead He said, "I tell you the truth, today you will be with me in paradise" (Luke 22:43). The translation "I tell you the truth today: you will be with me in paradise" is unnatural and forced.

What is paradise like? When people talk about heaven in casual conversation, they often think of it as a place where balding men in white robes strum harps while sitting on wispy clouds. That, however, is not the picture the Bible paints. The believer's final resting place has very definite attributes.

Jesus taught that those who believe in Him are bound for heaven and that the kingdom of heaven is near (Matt. 10:7). He told the ones He sent out to rejoice that their names were written in heaven (Luke 10:20). Paul reminded the Philippians that their citizenship was in heaven (Phil. 3:20). The word *heaven* is used 550 times in the Bible. We should therefore be able to obtain a very good picture of what heaven is like. It is real; it is not merely a wishful thought or a matter of idle speculation, though many people today find its reality difficult to believe. Scientific knowledge seems to have excluded the possibility of heaven. In astronomy, our radio telescopes have probed deep into space and have never found any evidence of pearly gates. There are no angels sitting on the clouds, and our receivers pick up no heavenly music. Nor have the electron microscopes and linear accelerators of the physicists picked up any evidence of heaven.

But is heaven a place that can be located by human technology? Even if we could penetrate the most distant realm by telescope and the smallest area by microscope, we could not prove that there is no heaven. It would take exhaustive knowledge to disprove its existence. If I want to show there isn't a needle in a nearby haystack, I must sift through the entire stack and not find one. If I want to show that there is, I merely need to find one.

The same is true with heaven. We have still explored so little of the universe that it is unreasonable to believe that science has disproved the existence of heaven. It is especially unreasonable when we consider the very real possibility that heaven is beyond the three dimensions we know. It is not a physical entity, but a spiritual one. We most likely could not discover its location by the use of scientific instruments. Rather we may only be able to know of its existence from someone who has been there and returned. And we have just that.

When Jesus rose from the grave, He gave the most reliable information about the afterlife we could have. His was not just resuscitation but a true resurrection from the dead. We can safely trust His testimony. Before He was crucified, He gave the disciples the following assurance of the reality of heaven: "In my Father's house are many rooms; if it were not so, I would have told you. I am going to prepare a place for you" (John 14:2). If heaven did not exist, He would have made it clear so they would not have the hope of eternal life. But He told them that it existed and was real.

Second, heaven is not far away. There is no dark river that must be crossed. There are no stages we must pass through in the afterlife to get to it. It is not at the end of a long period of soul sleep. It is close in time and perhaps also in proximity. Jesus' words "Today you will be with me in paradise" (Luke 23:43) seem to indicate immediacy of time and distance. The transfer to paradise is not a flight across the universe but may rather be as close to us as a fourth dimension.

Third, heaven is a permanent and eternal place. It is free from the possibility of change and defect. Perfection is the order of the day. The limitations of time and space, of death and disease, of disappointment and failure are no more. It is the eternal habitation of the believer. As Paul said to the Corinthian church, "Now we know that if the earthly tent we live in is destroyed, we have a building from God, an eternal house in heaven, not built by human hands" (2 Cor. 5:1).

Despite the thinking of some that heaven is merely a state

of mind, a fourth thing we can say is that it is rather a specific location. Jesus taught that He was going to prepare a *place* for His disciples (John 14:2). He told them to lay up treasures in heaven (Matt. 6:20). He refers to heaven as His Father's house (John 14:2). Many references speak of a city (Heb. 11:16; 13:14; Rev. 21:2). With verses like these heaven could not be simply a state of mind; it must be an actual place.

But though it is a place, it is not a limited place. Heaven is not limited by space or time. This, of course, is a difficult concept for us to understand. To imagine a world not limited by space or time is as difficult as it would be for someone living in a two-dimensional flatland to imagine three dimensions. But even if we were to consider heaven to be bound by physical space dimensions, it would nevertheless still not be a limited place. The Book of Revelation gives the dimensions of the Holy City as almost 1,500 miles on each edge of its cube (Rev. 21:16). This would make one side of the cube equal to half of the area of the continental United States. If we estimate that each story of the city to be fifteen feet high, the city would have 528 stories.

Whether we accept these as the actual dimensions of heaven or not, the significance of this number can be seen if we take the total square footage of the 528 stories (one trillion, one hundred eighty-eight billion square miles) and divide it by the estimated total population of the earth since the beginning of time (approximately 30 billion). The area left for each family would still be 198 square miles.[10] Thus, even using the numbers and estimates of a physical world, we have a picture of an uncrowded heaven.

A fifth attribute of heaven is beauty. Since it is where God dwells, we can easily imagine it to be a place of immense and astounding beauty. When John caught a vision of heaven, he used earthly symbols to try to explain the unexplainable. He said the walls were of jasper, and the city of pure gold, as pure as glass (Rev. 21:18). The foundations were precious stones and the gates pearl (Rev. 21:19–21). But these symbols are insufficient. Heaven is more beautiful than we can possibly imagine.

Service is a sixth feature of heaven. It is not a place of idleness as we might think from seeing cartoon spoofs of heaven. It is a place of creative activity that will be part of a believer's worship of God. With heightened powers of intellect and comprehension, he will render service to God and have full fellowship with Him (1 Cor. 13:12).

Heaven will be a glorious place for those who enter it. It will be home for those who seek it. But not all will find heaven. Jesus will reward those who believe in Him and share His glory with them (Rev. 3:12, 21). Those who reject His offer will not experience the joy of heaven. Each person must accept or reject Him.

When Jesus was confronted by Nicodemus, He said, "Unless a man is born again, he cannot see the kingdom of God" (John 3:3). However, when He was challenged by the disbelieving Pharisees, He said, "I am going away, and you will look for me, and you will die in your sin. Where I go you cannot come" (John 8:21). If we choose Jesus, we will go to heaven. If we reject Him, we will not.* He came to earth to die for our sins and redeem us (Rom. 3:24) so that whoever believes in Him would have a guarantee of eternal life (John 3:16).

But not all men choose to believe in Him. They reject what He has done for them and thus bring condemnation on themselves. As we read in John 3:17, "For God did not send his Son into the world to condemn the world, but to save the world through him." He does not condemn men. Rather, they con-

---

*Those who might wonder about the destiny of those who haven't heard or who can't believe are asked to turn to appendixes 2 and 3, pp. 173ff.

163

demn themselves. God "wants all men to be saved" (1 Tim. 2:4) and does not want "anyone to perish" (2 Peter 3:9). But unless man is willing to be reconciled to God (Rom. 5:10), he will spend eternity apart from Him.

Hell

The Bible informs us about hell as well as about heaven. Though many people think Jesus spoke only for paradise, that is not really the case. He actually spent more time talking about hell than He did about heaven. He taught that our actions on earth may put us in danger of the fire of hell (Matt. 5:22). He said that it is better to lose a part of the body than for the whole body to go to hell (Matt. 5:30; 18:9). He said that we should not fear those who can kill the body but that we should instead fear the one (God) who can destroy both body and soul in hell (Matt. 10:28; Luke 12:5). He asked the Pharisees how in their unbelief they could hope to escape being condemned to hell (Matt. 23:33). And He taught that the destination of the rich man who neglected to help Lazarus was hell (Luke 16:23).

The doctrine of hell is not a pleasant one, but it is nevertheless the teaching of the Bible. Many religions and cults, however, try to find some way to deny the existence or need of hell.

One way this is done is to teach that evil souls do not go to hell, but are instead destroyed. This is the doctrine of annihilation. The scriptural support for this doctrine usually comes from verses like Ecclesiastes 3:16–22. Though it is difficult to gain much support for the doctrine of annihilation from these verses, there is at least a hint of that teaching there. However, we must recognize that the context of this passage is very important. Ecclesiastes is written to teach the futility of any world view that is of human origin. The phrase "under the sun" is used to emphasize that the statements used in this section are typical of what could be learned by human wisdom alone (apart from revelation). Thus from the human perspective there is no hope of eternal life, and it appears that we go to extinction at death just as the animals do.

In contrast to this passage, which seems, at the surface, to teach annihilation, there are many that teach the reality of an *eternal* hell. A good example of this is Matthew 25:46: "Then they will go away to eternal punishment, but the righteous to eternal life." There are few who would argue that the verse does not teach an eternal life of bliss for the righteous. But if the verse teaches that for the righteous, then by the same logic it must also teach an eternal punishment for the unrighteous.

Verses like 2 Thessalonians 1:9 that use the word *destruction* might be thought of as arguing for annihilation but they do the opposite because they clearly speak of *everlasting* destruction. It is eternal, not temporal. Furthermore, the word *destruction* is best translated "ruin" (see the translation of the word *olethros* in 1 Thessalonians 5:3).

Such texts do not, in fact, teach annihilation, but rather eternal punishment. Though we might not like the conclusions that we must draw from Scripture, we must keep in mind that hell is where a person chooses to go if he rejects the provision God has made for him.

A second way the significance of hell is diminished is through the doctrine of purgatory. The Roman Catholic Church teaches that purgatory exists so that there might be temporal punishment to expiate the venial sins of the faithful who die. Though they cannot help themselves, others on earth can give them aid through their prayers and supplications, especially at appointed masses.

Though this may be a doctrine believed by a very large proportion of the Christian world, there is no scriptural support for it. There are three passages in the Catholic Bible that are generally used to support the doctrine of purgatory. The first is 2 Maccabees 12:43–45. Since the book is found in the Apocrypha and is not accepted by Protestant churches as inspired, we may choose to dismiss it. However, whether we accept it or not, the passage does not support the doctrine. It merely speaks about prayer for soldiers who died in idolatry. It does not mention the idea of purgatory at all.

The other two passages are in the New Testament. Matthew 12:32 indicates that the sin against the Holy Spirit "will not be forgiven, either in this age or in the age to come." Contrary to the teaching of some Catholic theologians, this verse does not indicate that other sins will be forgiven in the age to come. Furthermore, there is no reference to purgatory.

The second passage in the New Testament is 1 Corinthians 3:12–15. It says that the works of each believer will be tested by fire. This test will not take place in a place called purgatory but rather on the Day of Judgment, as the context clearly indicates.

In addition to the fact that there are no verses to support the doctrine of purgatory, there are many that conflict with it. The Bible teaches that man is sinful and separated from God, unable to help himself (Rom. 3:21–26; 7:14–20; Eph. 2:8–10). He is not saved by further punishment or works but by God's work through Jesus Christ on the cross (Rom. 7:21–25; Eph. 2:8–10; Tit. 3:4–7). To believe in a doctrine of purgatory, one must assume that Jesus' death on the cross was not sufficient and that He does not cleanse us from all sin as 1 John 1:7 clearly states He does. Further, Romans 5:1 teaches that the believer is justified by Jesus Christ and 2 Thessalonians 2:13 teaches that he is sanctified by the Holy Spirit rather than through the fires of purgatory.

There is little or no evidence supporting the idea of purgatory, and many verses contradict it. Many verses reveal the existence of heaven and hell (Pss. 1; 73; Dan. 12:2; Matt. 7:13–14, 24–27; 25:1–13, 31–46; John 3:16; 2 Thess. 1:8–10;

Rev. 20:11–15; 22:14–15). But none reveals the existence of purgatory.

Hell is real; it is the destination of those who reject God's provision for them. God does not want people to end up in hell, but He will not force them to take another road. G. K. Chesterton once remarked, "Hell is the greatest compliment God has ever paid to the dignity of human freedom."[11] God allows us to choose Him or reject Him as free moral agents.

If a person does not choose God, he will be separated from Him by a great chasm (Luke 16:26). The barrier of sin between him and God that existed in life will be magnified in eternity. His sins, which could have been forgiven while he was on earth, have become unforgivable at death. The envy, the jealousy, the stubbornness, and the rebellion that could have been removed now loom as large as eternity and permanently separate him from God.

Hell is not just a place of punishment; it is a place of escape from God's righteous glory. Dante in his *Divine Comedy* called it a "painful refuge."[12] It is a refuge for those who have rejected God and desired their sins instead. If they were to stand in the glory of God with their sins magnified by eternity, they would suffer an even more painful fate. Hell is as much a refuge as it is a place of punishment.

A Concluding Word

Throughout this book we have been looking at a variety of issues related to death. In the first chapter we looked at death; in the second, at dying; and in the third, at grief. Our examination of these near-death encounters was covered in the next three chapters. Finally, we covered the subject of the afterlife in the last two chapters and attempted to provide a biblical perspective of life beyond the grave.

It is my hope that the foregoing discussion has been informative, enlightening, and even challenging and that it will be more to you than just cognitive information. I hope you will take time to consider how this information applies to you and how you will apply it in your own situation.

APPENDIX ONE

REINCARNATION: DO I GO AROUND ONLY ONCE?

One of the most pervasive of non-Christian doctrines is the doctrine of reincarnation. It is basic to the teachings of Hinduism, Buddhism, Jainism, Taoism, and others. Many Western people also believe in it. It has influenced our own culture a great deal in the last few decades.

Reincarnation is the belief that the soul leaves one body at death and is reborn into another body. This belief is often tied to the notion of Karma, the belief that our actions in this life determine our status in the next. Good deeds result in a higher incarnation. Bad deeds result in a lower incarnation.

The evidence for this doctrine comes primarily from stories told by people who, while hypnotized, recount incidents from their former lives. Probably one of the earliest and best known cases is recounted in the book *The Search for Bridey Murphy*.[1] Under hypnosis Mrs. Virginia Tighe began to talk in an Irish brogue about her previous life as a red-haired colleen named Bridey Murphy. On further investigation, much of the story was found to be simply a collection of childhood memories pieced together by the unconscious mind while under hypnosis. Most of it came from Mrs. Tighe's childhood contact with Mrs. Corkell. Mrs. Corkell's maiden name was Bridey Murphy; she was Irish, and two of her sons had the same names as Mrs. Tighe's imaginary friends.[2]

More recent interest has developed in reincarnation as a form of treatment. As far back as the time of Edgar Cayce (a Kentucky-born psychic) there have been claims that ailments in this life were due to injuries inflicted in a previous life. Cayce would often analyze a person during self-hypnosis to find the origin of his problems. Blindness, for example, might be due to persecution in a previous life. Frigidity might be the result of wearing chastity belts during the Middle Ages.

Today there is a lot of interest in "past-lives" therapy. People like Dick Sutphen (author of *You Were Born Again to Be Together*) uses hypnosis to take people back to their supposed past lives to release subconscious anxiety.

How are we to evaluate these expressions of belief in reincarnation? First, there is no scientific evidence for reincarnation. In his article "The Evidence for Survival From Claimed Memories of Former Incarnations," Dr. Ian Stevenson lists eight alternative explanations for the evidence (including demon possession).[3] There is just not enough evidence to prove that reincarnation actually occurs. Evidence for it is even more difficult to verify than out-of-body experiences because there is a large subjective element in hypnosis. Furthermore, it is difficult to separate information that the person may have gained through normal means from that which might have come from a previous existence.

For example, under hypnosis one man began speaking in Oscan, a language spoken in Italy in the third century B.C. He was even able to write down an Oscan curse. Only later, during additional sessions of hypnosis, was it discovered that the man had recently looked at an Oscan grammar in the library. Several phrases had registered in his unconscious mind and found expression in the hypnotic state.[4]

Second, there is no support for reincarnation in the Bible. Only a few verses are even used to try to show that the Bible teaches reincarnation. The only plausible passage used to "prove" reincarnation is Matthew 17:10–13. Here it appears that Jesus is teaching that John the Baptist was a reincarnation of Elijah. This, however, cannot be the case for three important reasons. First, Elijah never died but rose directly into heaven (2 Kings 2:1–5). Second, Elijah himself appeared on the Mount of Transfiguration after John the Baptist's ministry (Matt. 17:1–3). Third, the reference to John the Baptist as Elijah merely fulfilled the prophecy that he would go forth "in the spirit and power of Elijah" (Luke 1:17). This is not the same as a reincarnation.

Apart from these few verses, which seem on the surface to teach reincarnation, there are many that directly deny it. Hebrews 9:27 teaches that "it is appointed for men to die once, and after this comes the judgment." Death is not followed by further incarnations but rather by a final judgment. The concept of Karma is also refuted by many verses like Ephesians 2:8–9, which says, "For it is by grace you have been saved, through faith—and this not from yourselves; it is the gift of God—not by works, so that no one can boast." Salvation is not achieved by an endless cycle of incarnations and good deeds. It is a result of the grace of God who made a provision for us to be saved by Christ's death on the cross.

APPENDIX TWO

WHAT ABOUT THOSE WHO HAVE NOT HEARD?

The question is often raised: What happens to those who haven't heard about Jesus and therefore cannot choose or reject Him?

The Bible does not give a complete answer to the question. But there are certain principles that are contained in the Bible; so, although we may not be totally dogmatic on this subject, neither can we say that we must be agnostic toward it. There is sufficient information given so that we can gain a good perspective on it.

First, God never intended anyone to be out of fellowship with Him. Heaven was intended to be man's destination. God is holy and loving and wants everyone to repent (Exod. 34:6-7; Jonah 4:10-11; 2 Peter 3:9). Though He is a just and righteous God, He is also a loving God.

Second, God's nature prevents Him from being unfair. The Bible teaches that God judges fairly (Gen. 18:25; Pss. 7:11; 9:18; 1 Peter 1:17). In His infinite justice, He will be much fairer than we with our limited understanding of justice could possibly be.

Third, man is not in total ignorance or spiritual darkness.

The Bible clearly teaches that man has an awareness both of God and of eternity (Ps. 19:1–4; Eccl. 3:11; John 1:9; Acts 14:15–17; Rom. 1:18–21; 2:15). It was the Roman sage Seneca who said, "God is near you, is with you. A sacred Spirit dwells within us, the Observer and Guardian of all our evil and all our good. There is no good man without God."[1]

However, this God-consciousness is not enough. Man must have more information than this in order to be saved. The Christian message is in jeopardy at either extreme. If God-consciousness is sufficient for salvation, then the Bible's revelation is unnecessary. This is wrong because the Bible places such an importance in bringing the message of Jesus Christ to those who have not heard (Rom. 10:14). But if the Bible is the *only* way a person can be saved, then we are back to our initial question about those who haven't heard.

In these cases, we have a fourth principle: God will provide the necessary information to those who seek Him. God rewards those who seek Him (Heb. 11:6). He will give anyone who earnestly seeks Him enough information to make a decision (1 Chron. 15:2; Ps. 9:10; Prov. 8:17; Jer. 29:13; Acts 8:30–31). God sent Peter to a Roman official named Cornelius to tell him about Jesus (Acts 10). It is also possible that God may work faith in a person's heart so that, like Job, he may say, "I know that my Redeemer lives," without knowing the identity of that Redeemer.

Fifth, the responsibility for a decision concerning this information belongs to each one of us. We are each ultimately responsible for the course we choose. No one can make the decision for us. As C. W. Hale Amos wrote, "From what we do know, respecting the terms of our own salvation, we are led irresistibly to the conclusion that no man can perish except by his own fault and deliberate choice."[2]

We do not have a complete answer to this question. The above principles indicate that God wants all of us to repent, that He is a fair judge, that He will give all of us enough information, and that we are responsible for the decision we make based on that information.

But there is not a totally clear picture about what happens to those who have not heard. This should give us all the more reason to make sure, if we are Christians, that we do what we can to share the Good News with all people or, if we are not Christians, we make a decision for Jesus Christ today. If we are not completely sure that we are believers, we should make sure by a conscious decision. As C. S. Lewis said in *Mere Christianity*, "If you are worried about the people outside [of Christianity], the most unreasonable thing you can do it to remain outside yourself."[3]

APPENDIX THREE

WHAT ABOUT
THOSE WHO
CANNOT BELIEVE?

When a young child dies the bereaved parents will often ask, "Where is my baby now? Will my child go to heaven?" As in the case of those who haven't heard (appendix 2), the Bible does not give us a definitive answer to these questions. However, several statements seem to indicate that heaven is the destiny of those who *can't* believe.

This question about those who can't believe differs however, from the question about those who have never heard in that it does not involve a consideration of whether God has provided sufficient information. Instead, the issue is what God will do in His justice to those who were not able, because of age or mental inability, to respond to His revelation. If they are saved, how are they saved and on what basis are they saved? Wouldn't the logic that says a child is saved say the same for an adult? In order to answer these questions, let us look at a few basic biblical principles.

First, God is loving (1 John 4:16), good (Nah. 1:7), just (Zeph. 3:5), compassionate, and gracious (Ps. 103:8). He "wants all men to be saved" (1 Tim. 2:4) and does not want "anyone to perish" (2 Peter 3:9). Therefore, it is inconceivable that God would damn an innocent child who is incapable of belief.

When we use the word *innocent* in this context we are not implying that the one who cannot believe is free from sin. The Bible clearly teaches that even infants inherit a sinful nature (Ps. 51:5; Rom. 5:12, 18–19). Their salvation comes not from being innocent from sin but rather from their ignorance of God's revelation.

Second, Christ's death on the cross for our sins was for all of us unless we refuse to accept it. God gives us the ability to decide. This means that we can either accept or reject God's love for us.

But what about those who are unable to accept or reject God? We must first realize that everyone (including those who cannot believe) is lost (Luke 19:10), perishing (John 3:16), condemned (John 3:18), and under God's wrath (John 3:36). We must also realize that Christ's death on the cross paid the debt of sin for us. His death appeases God's wrath (Rom. 5:9), and this provision is available to all unless they reject it. As Robert Lightner says in *Heaven for Those Who Can't Believe*, "Since rejection of the Savior is the final reason why men go to Hell, those who do not reject Him because they are not able to make a conscious decision enter Heaven on the basis of the finished work of Christ."[1]

Third, there are examples in the Bible that seem to support the notion that children who die are bound for heaven. In 2 Samuel 12:22–23 David learned of the death of his son by Bathsheba. In his relationship with Bathsheba David broke four of the Ten Commandments: he coveted, he stole, he committed adultery, and he committed murder. As punishment, his child was to die. However, when he learned that the child had died, he took heart that his son was in heaven. He said, "I will go to him, but he will not return to me."

In Luke 18:16–17, Jesus used children as an object lesson

for the kind of faith that leads to eternal life. He taught that the kingdom of God belongs to such as they (Luke 18:16) and that each believer must accept the kingdom of God as a little child (Luke 18:17). He further taught that God was "not willing that any of these little ones should be lost" (Matt. 18:14).

Fourth, there are no biblical references that even hint that children will be in hell. While there are many references to adults in hell, there are none to children. This is admittedly an argument from silence. But in other passages in which the context might warrant such a reference, none is found. Consider, for example the accounts of the death of mankind in the Flood (Gen. 7:21–23), the destruction of Sodom and Gomorrah (Gen. 19:24–25), the slaying of the firstborn in Egypt (Exod. 12:29–30), the destruction of the Amalekites (1 Sam. 15:3), and the slaying of the little boys in Bethlehem (Matt. 2:16).

The character of God is such that He would not damn to hell those who cannot believe. Further, Christ's death on the cross paid the debt of man's sin and is available to all unless they reject it. There are biblical examples to support the idea that children who die in infancy go to heaven. There is a total absence of verses that speak of children in hell. We can therefore declare with some certainty that those who cannot believe go to heaven when they die.

Let Christians in loving concern commit the world's children to the grace and mercy of God in prayer and commend the mentally impaired to His fatherly love.

NOTES

ONE

[1]Andrew Greeley, *Death and Beyond* (Chicago: Thomas More, 1976), p. 40.

[2]Arnold Toynbee, "Traditional Attitudes Towards Death," in *Man's Concern With Death*, ed. Arnold Toynbee et al. (New York: McGraw, 1968), p. 63.

[3]Ernest Becker, *The Denial of Death* (New York: Free, 1973).

[4]Kenneth L. Woodward, "How America Lives With Death," *Newsweek* (6 April 1970), pp. 81–88.

[5]W. Stekel, *Compulsion and Doubt* (London: Peter Nevill, 1950).

[6]Kenneth L. Woodward, "Living With Dying," *Newsweek* (1 May 1978), p. 61.

[7]Merrill Sheils, "Studying Death," *Newsweek* (14 March 1977), p. 43.

[8]Edwin S. Shneidman, "The Enemy," *Psychology Today* (August 1970), pp. 37–40, 62–66.

[9]"A Time to Write," *Time* (14 November 1977), pp. 94–96.

TWO

[1]Herman Feifel, "Attitudes Toward Death in Some Normal and Mentally Ill Populations," *The Meaning of Death*, ed. Herman Feifel (New York: McGraw, 1959), pp. 114–28.

[2]Paul R. Carlson, *Before I Wake* (Elgin, Ill.: David C. Cook, 1975), p. 29.

[3]Barney G. Glaser and Anselm L. Strauss, *Awareness of Dying* (Chicago, Ill.: Aldine, 1968).

[4]Jane Brody, "Dealing With Death: A Fact of Life," *Dallas Morning News* (3 December 1977).

[5]Daniel Goleman, "We Are Breaking the Silence About Death," *Psychology Today* (September 1976), pp. 44–47, 103.

[6]Elisabeth Kubler-Ross, "Dying as a Human-Psychological Event," in *The Experience of Dying*, ed. Norbert Greinacher and Alois Muller (New York: Herder and Herder, 1974), pp. 48–53.

[7]An understanding heart (1 Kings 3:9), a tender heart (2 Kings 22:19), and a compassionate heart (Col. 3:12) come from God.

[8]"Coping With Death in the Family," *Business Week* (15 April 1976).

[9]Cicely Saunders, *Care of the Dying* (London: Macmillan, 1959).

[10]Joseph Bayly, *The View From a Hearse* (Elgin, Ill.: David C. Cook, 1973), pp. 35–37.

[11]A. D. Weisman and T. P. Hackett, "Predilection to Death," *Psychosomatic Medicine* 23 (1961): 232.

[12]Kenneth L. Woodward, "Living With Dying," *Newsweek* (1 May 1978), p. 54.

[13]John M. Hinton, "Psychiatric Consultation in Patients With Fatal Illness," *Proceedings of the Royal Society of Medicine* (1972).

[14]John E. Schowalter, "The Child's Reaction to His Own Terminal Illness," in *Loss and Grief*, ed. Bernard Schoenberg et al. (New York: Columbia University Press, 1970), pp. 51–69.

[15]J. Robertson, "Some Responses of Young Children to the Loss of Maternal Care," *Nursing Times* 49 (1953): 382.

THREE

[1]Arnold Toynbee, "Traditional Attitudes Towards Death," in *Man's Concern With Death*, ed. Arnold Toynbee et al. (New York: McGraw, 1968), pp. 69–94.

[2]Sophocles in *Oedipus Coloneus*, lines 1224–26.

[3]Ernest Nagel, "Naturalism Reconsidered," in *Essays in Philosophy*, ed. Houston Peterson (New York: Pocket Library, 1954), p. 496.

[4]Richard T. Pienciak, "Just Leave Woody Allen Alone," *Dallas Morning News* (9 April, 1978), p. 6C.

[5]John Macmurray, *Person in Relation* (London: Faber and Faber, 1957), p. 165.

[6]Elisabeth Kubler-Ross, *Questions and Answers on Death and Dying* (New York: Macmillan, 1974).

[7]Paul R. Carlson, *Before I Wake* (Elgin, Ill.: David C. Cook, 1975), p. 19.

[8]Ibid., p. 20.

[9]Jane E. Brody, "Dealing With Death: A Fact of Life," *Dallas Morning News* (3 December 1977).

[10]Kenneth L. Woodward, "Living With Dying," *Newsweek* (1 May 1978), p. 53.

[11]Joseph Bayly, *The View From a Hearse* (Elgin, Ill.: David C. Cook, 1973), p. 58.

[12]Woodward, "Living With Dying," p. 56.

[13]Erich Lindemann, "Symptomatology and Management of Acute Grief," *American Journal of Psychiatry* 101 (1944): 141–48.

[14]The basic structure and outline of the steps of grief follows Granger E. Westberg's booklet *Good Grief* (Philadelphia: Fortress, 1971), though additions and deletions have been made as well.

[15]C. S. Lewis, *A Grief Observed* (New York: Bantam, 1961), p. 1.

[16]Joshua Loth Liebman, *Peace of Mind* (New York: Simon and Schuster, 1946).

[17]Bayly, *View From a Hearse*, pp. 55–56.

[18]Lewis, *A Grief Observed*, p. 67.

[19]"The Stages of Grief," *Christian Medical Society Journal* 5 (Fall 1974): 11–16.

[20]Marjorie Brumme, "How Not to be a Miserable Comforter," in *Death: Jesus Made It All Different*, ed. Miriam G. Moran (New Canaan, Conn.: Keats, 1977), pp. 101–4.

[21]John Hinton, *Dying* (New York: Penguin, 1972), p. 187.

[22]Toynbee, "Traditional Attitudes Towards Death," p. 60.

[23]Herman Feifel quoted in Woodward, "Living With Dying," p. 61.

[24]"Some Parents Treat Death Like Sex," *Dallas Times Herald* (2 November 1978), p. 4D.

[25]Robert A. Furman, "The Child's Reaction to Death in the Family," in *Loss and Grief*, ed. Bernard Schoenberg (New York: Columbia University Press, 1970), p. 72.

[26]M. H. Nagy, "The Child's Theories Concerning Death," *Journal of Genetic Psychology* 73 (1948): 3.

[27]S. Anthony, *The Child's Discovery of Death* (London: Kegan Paul, Trench & Trubner, 1940).

[28]Furman, "Child's Reaction to Death," p. 76.

[29]Bayly, *View From a Hearse*, p. 61.

[30]Furman, "Child's Reaction to Death," p. 80.

[31]Ibid., pp. 76–77.

[32]Ibid., p. 82.

[33]F. S. Caprio, "Ethnological Attitudes Toward Death," *Journal of Clinical Psychopathology* 7 (1946): 737; idem, "A Study of Some Psy-

chological Reactions During Prepubescence to the Idea of Death," *Psychiatric Quarterly* 24 (1950): 495.

[34]Furman, "Child's Reaction to Death," pp. 77–78.

[35]"Coping With Death in the Family," *Business Week* (15 April 1976).

[36]Furman, "Child's Reaction to Death," pp. 82–83.

[37]Hinton, *Dying*, p. 193.

[38]B. Schlesinger and A. Macrae, "The Widow and Widower and Remarriage," *Omega*, vol. 2, p. 10.

[39]"Coping With Death in the Family."

FOUR

[1]William Shakespeare, *Hamlet*, Act III, Scene I, 79–83.

[2]Cima Star, "To Write About Death, We Must Contemplate Our Own Death," in *Death and Ministry*, ed. J. Donald Bane et al. (New York: Seabury, 1975), p. 23.

[3]David Winter, *Hereafter* (Wheaton, Ill.: Harold Shaw, 1972), p. 5.

[4]Bayly, *The View From a Hearse* (Elgin, Ill.: David C. Cook, 1973), p. 19.

[5]Bertrand Russell, "A Free Man's Worship" in *Mysticism and Logic* (New York: Doubleday Anchor, 1957), pp. 44–45.

[6]A paraphrase of the composite experience described by Raymond A. Moody, Jr., *Life After Life* (New York: Bantam, 1975), pp. 21–23.

[7]John White, "What the Dying See," *Psychic* (September/October 1976), p. 40.

[8]Kenneth L. Woodward, "There Is Life After Death," *McCalls* (August 1976), p. 134.

[9]Moody, *Life After Life*, pp. 84–85.

[10]George G. Richie, *Return From Tomorrow* (Waco: Chosen, 1978).

[11]Karlis Osis and Erlendur Haraldsson, *At the Hour of Death* (New York: Avon, 1977), p. 29.

[12]Kenneth L. Woodward, "Life After Death?" *Newsweek* (12 July 1976), p. 41.

[13]Robert S. Morison, "Death: Process or Event?" *Death Inside Out*, ed. Peter Steinfels and Robert M. Veatch (New York: Harper and Row, 1975), p. 63.

[14]Henry Campbell Black, *Black's Law Dictionary* (St. Paul, Minn.: West, 1968).

[15]Lyall Watson, *The Romeo Error* (New York: Dell, 1974), pp. 39–40.

[16]"Even Death Not Permanent," *Dallas Morning News* (17 April 1977), p. 9A.

[17]David Hendin, *Death As a Fact of Life* (New York: Norton, 1973), p. 24.

[18]Ibid., p. 33.

[19]" 'Dead' Woman Clings to Life," *Dallas Times Herald* (7 April 1978), p. 2A.

[20]A. K. Mant, "The Medical Definition of Death" in *Man's Concern With Death*, ed. Arnold Toynbee et al. (New York: McGraw, 1968), pp. 13–24.

[21]Moody, *Life After Life*, pp. 147–50.

[22]Joan Kron, "The Out-of-Body Trip: What a Way to Go!" *New York Magazine* (27 December 1976–3 January 1977), p. 70.

FIVE

[1]Marshall Goldberg, "On the Other Hand: A Doctor Looks At Death" *Medical World News* (6 September 1974), p. 52.

[2]Karlis Osis, *Deathbed Observations by Physicians and Nurses* (New York: Parapsychology Foundation, 1961), p. 30.

[3]Raymond A. Moody, Jr., *Life After Life* (New York: Bantam, 1975), pp. 64–73.

[4]Russell Noyes, Jr. and Roy Kletti, "Depersonalization in the Face of Life-Threatening Danger: An Interpretation," *Omega* 7 (1976): 103–14.

[5]Kenneth L. Woodward, "There Is Life After Death," *McCalls* (August 1976), p. 138.

[6]Moody, *Life After Life*, pp. 61–62.

[7]C. M. Parkes, *Bereavement: Studies of Grief in Adult Life* (New York: International Universities Press, 1972).

[8]Noyes and Kletti, "Depersonalization," p. 109.

[9]Moody, *Life After Life*, pp. 72–73.

[10]Albert Heim, "Uber den Tod durch Absturz," *Jb. Schweiz. Alpendub,* quoted in *General Psychopathology,* tr. Karl Jaspers (Manchester, England: University Press, 1963).

[11]R. Fisher and G. M. Landon, "On the Arousal State-Dependent Recall of Subconscious Experience: Stateboundness," *British Journal of Psychiatry* 120 (1972): 159–72; S. A. K. Wilson, *Modern Problems in Neurology* (London: Arnold, 1928), chap. 4.

[12]Wilder Penfield, *The Mystery of the Mind* (Princeton, N.J.: Princeton University Press, 1975).

[13]Issac Asimov, *The Human Brain: Its Capacities and Functions* (Boston: Houghton Mifflin, 1963), pp. 325–26.

[14]An address by the late Lord Geddes to the Royal Medical Society in Edinburgh, 1937, quoted by Rosalind Heywood in *Man's Concern With Death*, ed. Arnold Toynbee (New York: McGraw, 1968), pp. 195–96.

[15]Edith Hamilton and H. Cairns, eds. *The Collected Dialogues of Plato* (New York: Bollingen Foundation, 1961).

[16]Plutarch, *On the Delay of Divine Justice,* quoted by Archie Matson in *The Waiting World* (New York: Harper and Row, 1975), p. 34.

[17]F. W. H. Myers, *Human Personality and Its Survival of Bodily Death* (New Hyde Park, N. Y.: University Books, 1961), pp. 212–17.

[18]F. S. Smythe, *The Spirit of the Hills* (London: Hodder, 1941), pp. 279–282.

[19]Stanislav Grof and Joan Halifax-Grof, "Psychedelics and the Experience of Death," in Arnold Toynbee et al., *Life After Death* (New York: McGraw, 1976), p. 196.

[20]Moody, *Life After Life*, p. 163.

[21]Celia Green, *Out-of-the-Body Experiences* (New York: Ballantine, 1968), p. 8.

[22]Joan Kron, "The Out-of-Body Trip: What a Way to Go!" *New York Magazine* (27 December 1976–3 January 1977), p. 72.

[23]Sigmund Freud, "Thoughts for the Times on War and Death," in *Collected Papers* 4 (New York: Basic Books, 1959), pp. 304–5.

[24]Noyes and Kletti, "Depersonalization."

[25]Michael Grosso, "Some Varieties of Out-of-Body Experience," *Journal of the American Society for Psychical Research* (April 1976), pp. 185–86.

[26]*Evangelical Newsletter* (November 4, 1977).

[27]John Rowan Wilson, *The Mind* (New York: Time-Life, 1969), p. 156.

[28]Stanislav Grof, "Varieties of Transpersonal Experiences: Observations from LSD Psychotherapy," *The Journal of Transpersonal Psychology* 4 (1972): 67.

²⁹Louis Jolyon West, "A Clinical and Theoretical Overview of Hallucinatory Phenomena," in R. K. Siegel and L. J. West, eds., *Hallucinations: Behavior, Experience, and Theory* (New York: Wiley, 1975), p. 292.

³⁰Kron, "Out-of-Body Trip," p. 68.

³¹Ronald K. Siegel and Murray E. Jarvik, "Drug-induced Hallucinations in Animals and Man," in R. K. Siegel and L. J. West, eds., *Hallucinations: Behavior, Experience, and Theory* (New York: Wiley, 1975), pp. 116–17.

³²Woodward, "There Is Life After Death," p. 136.

³³Ibid., p. 139.

³⁴Antoinette May, "Back From Beyond," *San Francisco Sunday Examiner & Chronicle* (10 April 1977), p. 16.

³⁵Ibid.

³⁶Ibid., pp. 16, 18.

³⁷Ibid., p. 18.

³⁸Robert Crookall, *Out-of-the-Body Experiences: A Fourth Analysis* (Secaucus, N. J.: Lyle Stuart, Citadell, 1977); Stanley Plumly, *Out-of-Body Travel* (West Menlo Park, Calif.: Echo, 1978); and others were written earlier by scientists involved in research in psychic phenomena and parapsychology.

³⁹Paul Twitchell, *Eckankar: The Key to Secret Worlds* (New York: Lancer, 1969), p. 123.

⁴⁰Kron, "Out-of-Body Trip," p. 71.

⁴¹John Palmer, "Consciousness Localized in Space Outside the Body," *Osteopathic Physician* (April 1974).

⁴²James C. Coleman, *Abnormal Psychology and Modern Life*, 5th ed. (Glenview, Ill.: Scott, Foresman, 1976), p. 471.

⁴³Daniel Goleman, "Back From the Brink," *Psychology Today* 11 (April 1977): 56–58.

⁴⁴Robert A. Monroe, *Journeys Out of the Body* (Garden City, N.Y.: Doubleday, Anchor Books, 1971), pp. 10–11.

⁴⁵Karlis Osis and Erlendur Haraldsson, *At the Hour of Death* (New York: Avon, 1977), p. 98.

⁴⁶Osis, *Deathbed Observations*, p. 68.

⁴⁷Osis and Haraldsson, *At the Hour of Death*, p. 29.

⁴⁸Karlis Osis quoted by Charles Panati in "Is There Life After Death?" *Family Circle* (November 1976), pp. 84, 90.

⁴⁹Sir William Barrett, *Death-bed Visions* (London: Methuen, 1926), p. 14.

[50]Quoted by Alson J. Smith from *Guideposts* in *Primer for the Perplexed* (New York: Day, 1962), p. 58.

[51]Maurice Rawlings, *Beyond Death's Door* (Nashville: Nelson, 1978), p. 21.

[52]David R. Wheeler, *Journey to the Other Side* (New York: Ace, 1977), pp. 116–19.

[53]Goleman, "Back From the Brink," p. 57.

[54]John White, "What the Dying See," *Psychic* (September–October 1976), p. 40.

[55]Osis, *Deathbed Observations*, p. 31.

[56]White, "What the Dying See," p. 40.

[57]Moody, *Life After Life*, p. 59.

[58]Osis, *Deathbed Observations*, p. 70.

[59]Woodward, "There Is Life After Death," p. 138.

[60]Moody, *Life After Life*, p. 59.

[61]Woodward, "There Is Life After Death," p. 136.

[62]Ibid., p. 97.

[63]Raymond A. Moody, Jr., *Reflections on Life After Life* (New York: Bantam, 1977), p. 111.

[64]Woodward, "Life After Death?" *Newsweek* (12 July 1976), p. 41.

[65]Woodward, "There Is Life After Death," p. 136.

[66]Kron, "Out-of-Body Trip," p. 68.

SIX

[1]Charles Panati, "Is There Life After Death?" *Family Circle* (November 1976), p. 78.

[2]Maurice Rawlings, *Beyond Death's Door* (Nashville: Nelson, 1978), p. 22.

[3]"Scientific Evidence for Life After Death," *Christianity Today* (27 August 1976), p. 21.

[4]William Gildea, "'Dead Man' Tells Startling Story of Life After Death," *Dallas Times Herald* (5 July 1977), p. 8B.

[5]Kenneth L. Woodward, "There Is Life After Death," *McCalls* (August 1976), p. 138.

[6]Alfred Edersheim, *The Life and Times of Jesus the Messiah* (Grand Rapids: Eerdmans, 1965), 2:324–25.

[7]Robert A. Monroe, *Journeys Out of the Body* (Garden City, N.Y.: Anchor, 1971), p. 175.

[8]E. Garth Moore, *Try the Spirits* (New York: Oxford University Press, 1977), p. 59.

[9]Robert Crookall, *Out-of-the-Body Experiences* (Secaucus, N.J.: Citadel, 1970), pp. 145–46.

[10]Ibid., pp. 147–48.

[11]Ibid., pp. 153–55.

[12]J. Vernon McGee, *Ecclesiastes and Song of Solomon* (Pasadena, Calif.: Thru the Bible Books, 1977), p. 90.

[13]Footnote in *Ryrie Study Bible* (Chicago: Moody), p. 998.

[14]Rosalind Heywood, "Attitudes to Death in Light of Dreams and Other Out-of-the-Body Experiences," in *Man's Concern With Death*, ed. Arnold Toynbee et al. (New York: McGraw, 1968), p. 210.

[15]Paul Edwards and Arthur Pap, eds., *A Modern Introduction to Philosophy*, 3rd ed. (New York: Free, 1973), p. 172.

[16]Mark P. Cosgrove, *The Essence of Human Nature* (Grand Rapids: Zondervan, 1976).

[17]"The Rediscovery of Human Nature," *Time* (2 April 1973), pp. 79–80.

[18]John White, "What the Dying See," *Psychic* (September–October 1976), p. 40.

[19]Karlis Osis and Erlendur Haraldsson, *At the Hour of Death* (New York: Avon, 1977), p. 7.

[20]Raymond Moody, quoted by Charles Panati in "Is There Life After Death?" *Family Circle* (November 1976), p. 84.

[21]Panati, "Is There Life After Death?" p. 90.

[22]Lennie Kronisch, "Elisabeth Kubler-Ross: Messenger of Love," *Yoga Journal* (November–December 1976), p. 20.

[23]Ann Nietzke, "The Miracle of Kubler-Ross," *Human Behavior* (September 1977), pp. 18–27.

[24]Mark Albrecht and Brooks Alexander, "Thanatology: Death and Dying," *Journal of the Spiritual Counterfeits Project* (1 April 1977), p. 8.

[25]Raymond A. Moody, Jr., *Life After Life* (New York: Bantam, 1975), p. 156.

[26]Gordon R. Lewis, "Criteria for the Discerning of Spirits," in *Demon Possession: A Medical, Historical, Anthropological and Theological Symposium*, ed. John Warwick Montgomery (Minneapolis: Bethany Fellowship, 1976), pp. 346–63.

[27]Robert A. Monroe, *Journeys Out of the Body*, pp. 138–39.

[28]Jane Roberts, *Seth Speaks* (New York: Bantam, 1972), pp. 141–42.

SEVEN

[1]Clifford A. Wilson, *Rocks, Relics, and Biblical Reliability* (Grand Rapids: Zondervan, 1977).

[2]C. S. Lewis, *Mere Christianity* (New York: Macmillan, 1952), pp. 55–56.

[3]Jon A. Buell and O. Quentin Hyder, *Jesus: God, Ghost, or Guru?* (Grand Rapids: Zondervan, 1978).

[4]Leslie Weatherhead's book *Life Begins at Death* is quoted by David Winter in *Hereafter* (Wheaton, Ill.: Harold Shaw, 1972), pp. 89–90.

[5]J. C. Pollock, *Moody* (New York: Macmillan, 1963), pp. 317–18.

[6]Maurice Rawlings, *Beyond Death's Door* (Nashville, Tenn.: Nelson Publishers, 1978), pp. 97–99.

[7]Two notable examples are Betty Malz in *My Glimpse of Eternity* (Waco: Word, 1978) and Marvin Ford in *On the Other Side* (Plainfield, N.J.: Logos, 1978).

[8]Raymond A. Moody, Jr., *Life After Life* (New York: Bantam, 1975), p. 140.

[9]John Dart, "Heaven or Hell?—Not the Burning Question It Used to Be," *Dallas Times Herald* (2 September 1978), p. 17.

[10]Ibid.

[11]M. B. Sabom and S. Kreutziger, "Near-death Experiences," *Journal of the Florida Medical Association* 64 (September 1977): 648–50.

[12]Michael B. Sabom and Sarah Kreutziger, "Near-death Experiences," *New England Journal of Medicine* 297 (10 November 1977): 1071.

[13]Ibid.

[14]Raymond A. Moody, Jr., *Reflections on Life After Life* (New York: Bantam, 1977), p. 15

[15]Ibid., p. 18.

[16]Ibid., p. 19.

[17]Karlis Osis, *Deathbed Observations by Physicians and Nurses* (New York: Parapsychology Foundation, 1961), p. 30.

[18]John White, "What the Dying See," *Psychic* (September–October 1976), p. 40.

[19]Moody, *Life After Life*, p. 139.

[20]F. W. H. Myers, *Human Personality and Its Survival of Bodily Death* (Hyde Park, N.Y.: University Books, 1961), pp. 212–17.

[21]Rawlings, *Beyond Death's Door*, pp. 17–21.

[22]Thomas Welch, *Oregon's Amazing Miracle* (Dallas: Christ for the Nations, 1976), pp. 7–10.

EIGHT

[1]T. S. Eliot, "The Hollow Men" (1925).

[2]Kenneth L. Woodward, "Life After Life?" *Newsweek* (1 May 1978), p. 63.

[3]John Haynes Holmes, "Ten Reasons for Believing in Immortality" in *A Modern Introduction to Philosophy*, ed. Paul Edwards and Arthur Pap, 3rd ed. (New York: Free, 1973), pp. 253–54.

[4]David Winter, *Hereafter* (Wheaton, Ill.: Harold Shaw, 1972), p. 46.

[5]Hal Lindsey, *The Terminal Generation* (Old Tappan, N.J.: Revell, 1976), pp. 91–97.

[6]J. N. D. Anderson, *The Evidence of the Resurrection* (Downers Grove, Ill.: InterVarsity Press, 1966); Josh McDowell, *Evidence That Demands a Verdict* (San Bernardino, Calif.: Campus Crusade for Christ, 1972); Frank Morison, *Who Moved the Stone?* (Grand Rapids: Zondervan, 1977).

[7]Winter, *Hereafter*, p. 30.

[8]Robert Ervin Hough, *The Christian After Death* (Chicago: Moody, 1947), p. 60.

[9]Ibid., pp. 31–33.

[10]Ibid., pp. 111–12.

[11]G. K. Chesterton, quoted by Leighton Ford in *Christ the Liberator* (Downers Grove, Ill.: InterVarsity Press, 1971).

[12]Dante, *Inferno*, Scene V: 16.

APPENDIX 1

[1]Morey Bernstein, *The Search for Bridey Murphy* (Garden City, N.Y.: Doubleday, 1956).

[2]Martin Gardner, *Fads and Fallacies in the Name of Science* (New York: Dover, 1957).

[3]Ian Stevenson, "The Evidence for Survival From Claimed Memories of Former Incarnations," *Journal of the American Society for Physical Research* vol. 54, no. 2 (April 1960).

[4]Harold Rosen, *A Scientific Report on "The Search for Bridey Murphy"* (New York: Julian, 1956).

APPENDIX 2

[1]Quoted in J. Oswald Sanders, *How Lost Are the Heathen?* (Chicago: Moody, 1972), p. 53.

[2]Ibid., p. 54.

[3]C. S. Lewis, *Mere Christianity* (New York: Macmillan, 1972), p. 50.

APPENDIX 3

[1]Robert P. Lightner, *Heaven for Those Who Can't Believe* (Schaumburg, Ill.: Regular Baptist Press, 1977), p. 20.

AUDIOVISUALS

CASSETTE TAPES

Coping with Death and Dying: Emotional Needs of the Dying Patient and the Family. Talks by Dr. Elisabeth Kubler-Ross, 1973. Produced and distributed by Ross Medical Associates, S.C., 1825 Sylvan Court, Flossmoor, IL 60422.

The five thirty-minute tapes discuss the verbal and nonverbal language of death, the stages of dying, children and death, and sudden death.

Death, Grief, and Bereavement. Twenty-four tapes from 21 to 59 minutes long, 1972–1975. Available from the Charles Press Publisher, Bowie, MD 20715.

These tapes were initially produced and distributed by the Center for Death Education and Research and deal with a wide variety of topics on death, dying, grief, and bereavement.

Death in the Family. Talk by Eda LeShan. Distributed by *Psychology Today*, Department ST9, P.O. Box 278, Pratt Station, Brooklyn, NY 11205.

The author of "Learning to Say Goodbye" discusses the emotional and psychological trauma we experience when a close relative dies. Focusing on the anger, guilt, grief, and loneliness of children, she explains how to help them cope with the loss.

Death, the Enemy. Talk by Edwin S. Shneidman. Distributed by *Psychology Today*, Department ST9, P.O. Box 278, Pratt Station, Brooklyn, NY 11205.

This noted thanatologist examines death and dying and discusses the role of the individual in his own death. He also discusses suicide, the survivor's reaction to death, the fear of death, and theories about the process of death.

FILMSTRIPS

Perspective on Dying. Filmstrip with record or cassette of six programs with instructor's manual, role-playing cards, questionnaire, and text, 1973. Produced and distributed by Concept Media, 1500 Adams Avenue, Costa Mesa, CA 92626.

The six programs are: American Attitudes Toward Death and Dying, Psychological Reactions of the Dying Patient, Hazards and Challenges in Providing Care, Guidelines for Interacting with the Dying Person, The Dying Patient, and The Nurse.

FILM

If I Should Die. Forty-five minute color film produced by Evangelical Films, 1978, 2848 W. Kingsley, Garland, TX 75041.

A docu-drama film that deals with views of death in our culture, afterlife experiences, grief, and bereavement. Much of the film is devoted to interviews with Christian psychologists, doctors, and theologians on various aspects of death.

Though I Walk Through the Valley. Thirty-minute color film produced in 1972 and distributed by Pyramid Films, Box 1048, Santa Monica, CA 90406.

Filmed during the last few weeks of the life of a middle-aged college professor dying of cancer, this film explores the pain of death. The professor and his family discuss their feelings about his illness, his impending death, and their faith in God.

FOR FURTHER READING

GENERAL

Choron, Jacques. *Death and Modern Man.* New York: Collier, 1964.

Choron examines some of the philosophical questions raised about the meaning and purpose of life by the presence of death. He cites much of the work done by philosophers, physiologists, and psychiatrists concerning the human fear of death and the remedies people devise to counteract this fear.

Choron, Jacques. *Death and Western Thought.* New York: Collier, 1963.

The author surveys the thoughts of the great philosophers on the subject of death, and offers what he feels is the Christian answer to death.

Toynbee, Arnold, et al. *Man's Concern With Death.* New York: McGraw, 1968.

In this frequently cited book, Arnold Toynbee and others look at the subject of death from the viewpoint of their own specialty—medicine, psychiatry, theology, philosophy, anthropology, literature, and psychic research.

DYING

Feifel, Herman, ed. *New Meanings of Death.* New York: McGraw, 1977.

This book is an update of the classic The Meaning of Death *published in 1959. Contributions by researchers in the field are grouped under the following sections: Developmental Orientations, Clinical Management, The Survivors, and Responses to Death.*

Kubler-Ross, Elisabeth. *On Death and Dying.* New York: Macmillan, 1969.

This classic book in the field of thanatology summarizes the work of Dr. Kubler-Ross with over two hundred dying patients. The book contains a great deal of information, including a thorough description of the five stages of dying. Additional helpful material is found in the transcribed interviews with patients and an eleven-page bibliography.

Kubler-Ross, Elisabeth. *Questions and Answers on Death and Dying.* New York: Macmillian, 1974.

This sequel to Dr. Kubler-Ross's first book deals with many of the most frequently asked questions. Chapters deal with such subjects as dying patients, sudden death, funerals, and old age.

Shneidman, Edwin S., ed. *Death: Current Perspectives.* Palo Alto, Calif.: Mayfield, 1976.

This is a collection of forty reprinted articles and excerpts from books. They have been assembled into four sections focusing on cultural, societal, interpersonal, and personal perspectives on death.

Weisman, Avery D. *On Dying and Denying: A Psychiatric Study of Terminology.* New York: Behavioral Publications, 1972.

Weisman's book on dying is based on clinical material from hospitalized patients. It deals with some of the common misconceptions about death, dying, and the dying patient. It also explains aspects of denial, acceptance, and death.

DEATHBED AND AFTERLIFE EXPERIENCES

Moody, Raymond A., Jr. *Life After Life.* New York: Bantam, 1976.

First published in 1975 by Mockingbird, this book quickly became a bestseller for Bantam. Though not the first of its kind, it did attract attention to the afterlife reports of those who had "died" and returned.

Moody, Raymond A., Jr. *Reflections on Life After Life.* New York: Bantam, 1977.

As a sequel to the highly successful Life After Life, *this book adds a bit of new information, including four elements common to the experience of dying. It also notes that there are experiences that correlate with traditional views of the afterlife reflected in the Bible.*

Osis, Karlis and Erlendur Haraldsson. *At the Hour of Death.* New York: Avon, 1977.

Osis and Haraldsson give a good survey of the evidence from deathbed observations for survival after death. As an update of an original study titled Deathbed Observations by Physicians and Nurses, *it is one of the more scientific studies done by those involved in psychic research.*

Rawlings, Maurice. *Beyond Death's Door*. Nashville: Nelson, 1978.

Written by a cardiologist who has brought people back from death. The book is full of anecdotes and stories about those who have had both pleasant and unpleasant afterlife experiences.

Swihart, Phillip J. *The Edge of Death*. Downer's Grove, Ill.: Inter-Varsity, 1978.

Dr. Swihart, a clinical psychologist, examines the work of Dr. Elisabeth Kubler-Ross, Dr. Raymond Moody, and Robert Monroe on the afterlife. After looking at their studies, he provides an evaluation of the work from a Christian perspective and draws a number of insightful conclusions.

Wright, Rusty. *The Other Side of Life*. San Bernardino, Calif.: Here's Life Publishers, 1979.

One of the most thorough and scientific analyses by any Christian author. It deals with afterlife experiences and shares the Christian hope of salvation and life after death.

THE BIBLICAL VIEW OF DEATH AND DYING

Davidson, Glen W. *Living with Dying*. Minneapolis: Augsburg, 1975.

As Chief of Thanatology at the Southern Illinois University School of Medicine, Davidson has had the personal experience necessary to describe the process of dying. His perceptive writing and sensitive style provide the reader with insight into the needs of dying patients and their families.

Winter, David. *Hereafter*. Wheaton, Ill.: Harold Shaw, 1972.

This book, though more devotional than academic, does provide interesting information on both death and dying. It answers questions like: What happens when I die? What kind of body? and What is heaven like?

THE BIBLICAL VIEW OF THE AFTERLIFE

Hendriksen, William. *The Bible on the Life Hereafter*. Grand Rapids: Baker, 1959.

This is a very scholarly and comprehensive book on the subjects of personal eschatology (death and afterlife) and general eschatology (last days). It deals with subjects like communication with the dead, purgatory, soul sleep, heaven, and hell.

Zodhiates, Spiros. *Life After Death?* Ridgefield, N. J.: AMG, 1977.

Zodhiates has written what is probably one of the better popular books on the theology of death. It is divided into thirty-eight small chapters, each dealing with a specific question. It is well written and well documented.

GRIEF

Bayly, Joseph. *The View From a Hearse.* Elgin, Ill.: David C. Cook, 1973.

Bayly writes this book not only as a scholar but as a participant. Having lost three sons to death, he knows well the pain of grief. In this book he deals with both theoretical ideas (What is death? What is it like?) and practical suggestions (how to explain death to a child; how to cope with grief).

Lewis, C. S. *A Grief Observed.* New York: Bantam, 1961.

This book, republished by Bantam, is a collection of thoughts written by C. S. Lewis in his journal shortly after his wife of four years died. Originally published under a pseudonym—perhaps because it contains so many doubts about God and His grace—it eloquently demonstrates the strength of Christian faith in times of grief.

Moran, Mirian G., ed. *Death: Jesus Made It All Different.* New Canaan, Conn.: Keats, 1977.

A compilation of articles by such people as J. I. Packer, John Stott, Elisabeth Elliot, Norman Geisler, Ray Stedman, C. Everett Koop, and Joseph Bayly.

Morris, Sarah. *Grief and How to Live With It.* New York: Grosset and Dunlap, 1972.

A short booklet written by a woman who could not find a book like this on the subject of grief. It is very practical in its suggestions to those in grief and to those who desire to aid someone in grief.

Vanauken, Sheldon. *A Severe Mercy.* San Francisco: Harper and Row, 1977.

A true story about a husband and wife who love each other deeply, the death of one, and the pain of the other. In his time of greatest need he turned to his friend at Oxford, C. S. Lewis, for counsel and encouragement. The story of his wife's death and his correspondence with C. S. Lewis is a portrait of the conquering possibilities of faith and love.

Westberg, Granger E. *Good Grief.* Philadelphia: Fortress, 1971.

Written by a Lutheran clergyman on the faculty of the University of Illinois Medical School, this is an excellent book for those passing through the stages of grief. It depicts ten stages of grief and helps the reader to know what to expect and how to cope with grief at each stage.

BIBLIOGRAPHIES

Fulton, Robert, ed. *A Bibliography on Death, Grief, and Bereavement 1845–1973.* 3rd rev. ed. Minneapolis: University of Minnesota Center for Death Education and Research, 1973.

Kubler-Ross, Elisabeth. *On Death and Dying.* New York: Macmillan, 1969.

An eleven-page bibliography can be found at the back of the book.

Sell, Irene L. *Dying and Death: An Annotated Bibliography.* New York: Tiresias, 1977.

Watson, Lyall. *The Romeo Error.* New York: Dell, 1974.

A bibliography of over three hundred references can be found at the back of this book.

SCRIPTURE INDEX